HOW THE REFORMATION
HAPPENED

HOW THE REFORMATION HAPPENED

by
HILAIRE BELLOC
Author of
"TOWNS OF DESTINY," "THE CONTRAST," "ESTO PERPETUA"
etc.

DODD, MEAD & COMPANY, INC.

PRINTED IN THE UNITED STATES OF AMERICA

APOLLO EDITION

CONTENTS

CONTENTS

HOW THE REFORMATION HAPPENED

INTRODUCTORY

The Problem

Two historical problems are of prime importance to our race. To understand them sufficiently is to understand ourselves. To misapprehend them is to misapprehend our own nature: what made our culture and what threatens to destroy it.

The first of these problems is the Conversion of the Roman Empire to Catholicism. "How came the Pagan world to be baptized? What made Christendom?" The second is the disaster of the sixteenth century. "How came Christendom to suffer shipwreck? What made the Reformation?"

It is the second of these questions which I here approach.

Neither can be completely answered; for these vast spiritual changes come of powers outside our experience: Heaven and Hell are at work. But an adequate answer may be given, sufficient to make the great event comprehensible. Its main lines may be so presented that they fall into a right perspective, and we can say: "I now see how the thing happened. The human motives, at least, though their spiritual roots remain hidden, are clear and appear in their right order of importance. The surrounding circumstances in which they worked explain the results. The Picture is rational and, within its limits, true."

Now such an explanation of the affair is not presented to the modern mind by its accepted historians. The relation as given does not make sense: or only seems to do so if the reader is ignorant of the Catholic Church.

For the matter with which any story of the Reformation deals is the Catholic Church. The world upon which the Reformation fell and which it in part destroyed was the creation of the Catholic Church acting as a leaven for fifteen hundred, as a world-wide authority for a thousand, years. The Reformation was an attack on that institution; its fruit, called Protestantism, is a negative product of that institution: the principle of unity in that fruit is reaction against that institution: therefore is full knowledge of the institution essential to knowledge of the conflict. Yet the general histories upon which opinion has been mainly nourished missed the very stuff with which they were dealing, because they proceeded from authors who had no intimacy with the Catholic Church: who did not know "what it was all about."

It is not a point of sympathy or dislike. A man may truly relate a battle whether he applaud or deplore its issue. But he cannot relate it truly if he does not know the ground. A man writing three

Introductory

centuries hence of Victorian England might love or
hate its village life, but if he shall be all at sea on the
gentry and their villages he will be writing equally
bad history in praise or in blame of them. Whether
he supports or denounces the despotism of the squires
he will be worthless as an historian because the Victorian squires were not despots.

The two sources from which such histories have in
the main proceeded are the Academies of Protestant
culture in the North, of Anti-clerical in the South:
each (in very different ways) out of touch with their
material. Any brief list of half a dozen names at
random are enough to establish that truth: Michelet,
Macaulay, Ranke, Carlyle, Sismondi. Because neither
set of writers knows the material with which he is
dealing the Reformation seems to each a simple process with no problem to be solved. It is the man
really acquainted with Catholicism who finds the
difficulty of understanding the Reformation so great,
its riddle so nearly insoluble. Just as a man penetrated
with the high Pagan culture can hardly conceive its
transfiguration into the Christian Empire at the approach of the Dark Ages, so a man conscious of what
was (in part) destroyed at the Reformation is stag-
gered by the mere possibility of such destruction: he
knows what was lost; the facile historian of the Protestant sort on the one hand, of the Anti-clerical on
the other, does not.

To the first, the man of Protestant culture, the
process leading to the Reformation seems obvious.

How the Reformation Happened

From a variety of causes knowledge vastly expanded at the close of the Middle Ages. Geographical discoveries followed each other rapidly and on a new scale of greatness, a true idea was acquired of the earth and heavens, arts improved; at the same time Antiquity was re-discovered, original manuscripts were closely examined, a science of history began. The period is known as "The Renaissance," the "New Birth" of Europe. Under such an influence the Myths of a thousand uncritical years were exposed and dissolved. The institutions founded on these myths (the Papacy, the Mass, reliance on imagined influences of shrine and relic) were sapped, and with them crumbled all the society they informed.

Since men could not be expected to shed at once the religious influence of ten centuries, certain fragments of irrational mood survived, but they were increasingly rationalised. The Eucharist was retained as a form, but adversely discussed and more and more explained away. The Incarnation followed the same road, until the awful figure of a God Apparent faded into that of a mild young man at a loss. The successive liberations of the mind from illusion, left man more and more himself, like a successive stripping of veils. The old Catholic vesture was, indeed, retained by some of the more cultivated: but this retention was due either to their cowardice, their interest, or their routine, and the continued practice of superstitions in large societies was due to their racial inferiority worked on by persecuting governments which forbade enquiry.

Among the higher types, when all the alien, infused Catholicism had dissolved, the Essential Fellow appeared, the Complete Man, and turned out to be in the Germanies an East Elbe Prussian, in England a well-to-do Englishman, but in the United States a citizen of the United States.

The results to which such history would lead were soon reached. The great national figures of the Middle, the Dark, and even the Pagan ages became as it were Nature's Protestants. They may not have realised it fully at the time, but at the core Arthur, Penda, Offa, Arminius (more properly Hermann), Theodoric, Alfred, Otto, Edward I, were of that material. History was "read backwards" with a vengeance; and the Reformation could present no problem because it was but the final and necessary emergence of what had always been present below the surface in the noble ancestry of the writer.

Of *what* the thing they had lost might be these historians know nothing; and there is one major test among a thousand which can be unfailingly applied. To a man acquainted with the Catholic Church and the society it produces, nothing is clearer than that the plays of Shakespeare were written by a man steeped in Catholic social tradition and for audiences in the same mood. Yet so simple and obvious a truth sounds absurd in the ears of men who attempt to write of the Reformation without knowing what the Catholic Church may be.

But the difficulty of explaining the Reformation, the Problem it involves, is hardly better grasped by the historian of the second type, the sceptical or atheist historian, writing as from within the nations of Catholic culture, notably the French or Italian.

To these men Catholicism seems a phase of thought present among their ancestry, natural to their blood, creative in its day, but now exposed as demonstrably false. It lamely survives to-day—principally in women—through a mere adhesion to traditional and homely things. It is also supported politically (but without conviction) by those who act from affection for the past, from a fear of disorder, or from mere interest. Its life, however, has departed. The Church is a corpse.

This kind of historical writer does not conceive of the past in terms of the present; he does not "read history backwards," nor is he necessarily warped by hatred. Some, indeed, of his sort are spoiled by a spirit of mere antagonism, but the greater part—on account of their early memories, of their friendships, of the Catholic air about them, and of unbroken social traditions from the past—have, for at least some portion or another of the Catholic scheme, a real affection (much what a grown-up man would feel for the mixture of strong emotions with illusions in his boyhood).

To them the Protestantism produced by the

Introductory

Reformation is ridiculous and intellectually con-
temptible—far lower than the Catholic past—and
they despise the Protestant culture of to-day. Yet
that the united Catholic scheme of Europe should
have broken up in the sixteenth century seems to
them inevitable; its loss they regard as an advantage
to mankind, though they smile at the odd (now ending) interval of Bible worship and the rest. Though,
then, such Continental "Anti-clericals" are far better fitted to deal with European historical problems
than writers of Protestant culture (who are out of
the main stream), yet they also find the problem of
the Reformation easily solved—only because they do
not know in what terms it should be stated.

That they are indeed thus unable to state the Problem is apparent under a number of tests, of which
these may be considered:

They are not only bewildered and exasperated by
the recrudescence of Catholicism to-day but they
give wrong explanations for it: they call it a fad, an
hypocrisy, a decadent fashion, though the character
of the new recruits is glaringly at variance with such
bad judgment. The verse and prose, the attitude in
war, the triumphant irony, the sacrifices of those re-
turning to the faith to-day in the countries of Catholic culture, are manifestly the product of a mood not
only sincere but strong, not only strong but lucid,
not only lucid but well armed; and it is in this last
point that the anti-clerical historian most shows his
lack of touch with reality, for it is *intellectually* that

those whom he wildly calls "Neo-Catholics" (their Catholicism being one with St. Bernard's or St. Augustine's) are proving his superiors.

Again, this sort of anti-clerical writer did and does not follow the true historical order of events—and that is a capital weakness in men of his trade. He imagined a false sequence. He saw the non-Catholic writers of the seventeenth century—and especially those in the anti-Catholic side of Europe—as the originators of popular sovereignty, the first to state clearly the metaphor of contract in society or the principles of communal authority. He did not know that they derived from the great Suarez. He imagined the new science of the Renaissance as the root of a later Scepticism. He did not see the strong presence of Scepticism *before* the advance of knowledge in the field of physical science, nor appreciate the significance of Faith especially lively among the chief discoverers in that field.

Again (another grave weakness in his trade) he did not read the key-points: he despised and neglected those writings which would have explained to him the formation of that very culture from which he proceeded. Your anti-clerical historian of the nineteenth century had not read a line of St. Thomas, he was ignorant of the fundamental debates permanently necessary to all philosophy and never so vigorous as in the medieval schools. He missed the essential conflict of Nominalism and Realism. He knew not how all morals, property, authority, the diverse forms of government, had been analysed to exhaustion by those whom he left aside as unworthy of his attention. To take but one minor instance—a most illuminating one—he thought he could rely on the *Provinciales* of Pascal as the last word in a certain debate. He had never seen one page of Escobar's questions in the original:—what is worse, he did not know that Pascal was under the same disability.

This sort of anti-clerical writer, then, explained the Reformation easily because he explained it wrongly. He saw it as a necessary phase in the general exodus of our race from darkness into light: a phase confused and full of contradiction, ridiculous superstitions, and savage fanaticism, but suffering all these inevitably as part of a great revolution which was to end in a stable and happy society.

But he was all wrong. The vision of progress was in his mind alone, not in the real world. The Reformation did not continue a direct Renaissance tendency towards larger things, it deflected that tendency. It did not introduce the arts, it cramped and thwarted them. Its last effects have not led to a society happy or stable, they have led to the society we see around us to-day.

These older schools which found the great upheaval as inevitable as it was easily explicable have lately lost much of their weight. The puzzle of the Reformation is presenting itself with added force to-day, in our generation, which has seen the last traces of Protestant dogma—not ethics—disappear—

save perhaps, from some backwaters, such as Dayton in Tennessee.

Our generation lives in a world where Catholicism is the sole surviving positive force, where there surrounds that force a wide belt not Catholic, but in varying degrees of sympathy with Catholicism, while outside and beyond is a wreckage of philosophies inclining to despair.

It is to the Catholic or at least to the man who knows what Catholicism is (that is, to the man in the very heart of European tradition), to the man who knows fully *what* it was that was abandoned, to the man who can feel the profound void, and the quality of the loss involved by the Reformation, that its full problem appears.

He knows the balance, the satisfaction, the fullness of that which was rejected. How on earth came it ever to be rejected for such grotesque and petty aberrations as the various sects indulged in on its disappearance? Why, when that fever passed, did its effects remain? Why was manifest good allowed to perish?

One who found Greek sculpture dull, barbaric stuff would see no problem in its degradation and destruction in the failure of the Empire. But a man who knows what Greek sculpture is has a very different problem before him. He must try to understand how a thing so manifestly excellent, satisfactory to our civilised sense, ennobling, could have been left aside.

Introductory

The Catholic can easily understand how there should arise an indifference towards Catholic practice, or even a reaction of hatred against official Catholic action and individual Catholic authorities; but what remains for him a problem still unsolved is how that which was the very nature of Europe, and surely necessary to the European mind; that in which it had been nurtured and which was intimately itself —so that European and Catholic meant the same thing and so that "civilisation," "Occidental," "Catholic" all meant the same thing—should have its own *being* utterly rooted out of it in certain regions, and an original, stable character, happy because it was in tune with itself, transformed into a new, uneasy and unhappy thing which yet preferred to remain so transformed. *That* is the problem; *that* is the difficulty.

It hardly ever happens to the individual to-day. A person arriving at maturity in Catholic surroundings may grow hostile to authority or (more frequently) indifferent in practice; but he will hardly ever develop a general distaste for all the Catholic atmosphere and social tradition, still less an active hatred of them. Such an exceptional case would be like a loss of memory, or one of those strange phenomena which pathologists now and then discover in neurotic subjects.

Yet exactly that thing did happen to great groups of Europeans from three to four centuries ago, and what we have to try, in part at least, to explain is how so astonishing a revolution and loss of personality was made possible: and in so many places actually achieved and made permanent.

That is the problem. That is the question for which we may have to try to find an answer.

I have said that no complete answer can be given, but at least the right sequence of political causes and their right proportion may be presented in a sketch of that fatal century, and that is what I shall attempt in what follows.

I shall begin by describing how, as the last of so many perils, United Christendom was growing unstable during the three generations between the Black Death and the early sixteenth century, that is, between 1350 and 1500.

I shall come next to the sudden flood of that revolt in the German state and cities after 1517 and its spread elsewhere: a thing made possible by the constitution of Germany and especially by the invasion of the Turks.

Next, I shall present that strange fatality, the political Accident whereby England, hitherto the least affected of all Christian Provinces, was, under no popular pressure and without the will or knowledge of the policy's own Author, turned face about to join the new alien movement. The dissolution of the monasteries in 1536 to 1540, an act not connected in its author's mind with doctrine, proves the indirect cause of all that came after.

Then follows the mighty effect of Calvin, whose

book, character and organisation provided form and substance for Protestantism, and gave it personal being: for Calvin's mind was a portent and became the power directing the storm.

Under his effect the opposing forces prepare—1547-9 to 1559—for conflict throughout the west.

A universal battle of which France is the main field rages undecided from 1559 to 1572, covering all the west—Netherlands, England, Scotland—until, at the end of this, its first phase of active conflict, the final positions begin to appear: England and Scotland, the Northern Netherlands maintained in separation; France permanently divided but the Dynasty and the bulk of the nation rallying to the traditions of Europe.

The second phase of the great conflict—1572 to the end of the century—is but a confirmation of the new religious frontiers. The Battle has ended in a Draw which leaves Europe permanently divided upon the lines it has since preserved.

There is a belated attempt, indeed, in the next century, 1618-1648, made by the Emperor, to recover the many states and cities of Germany for Unity and to establish his own authority and the Ancient religion over all. It ends, through the genius of Richelieu—the Conductor of French policy—in a failure. Germany remains divided, but not before the struggle (the Thirty Years' War) has ruined German wealth and population for a century.

After that date (the peace of Westphalia in 1648)

the main struggle is at an end throughout Europe, and the effects of the Reformation are established.

The Advent of Disaster

The first thing we have to do in approaching our subject, if we are to get it in the right historical perspective, is to be rid of a certain illusion which the time and place in which we live naturally foster. It is the illusion that the Catholic Church lived a peaceable, equal life of unquestioned power throughout the centuries between the conversion of the Roman Empire and the great catastrophe of the sixteenth century.

It did nothing of the sort. It lived in perpetual conflict, and in perpetual peril, humanly speaking, of dissolution. It was perpetually under the assault of enemies from within and from without. And the reason is simple: it is not of the world.

The final shipwreck of European unity at the Reformation—if, indeed, it be final—was but the closing episode of a long voyage, in which shipwreck had been a present menace throughout.

The reason that the time and place in which we live (I mean we Catholics of Great Britain and of the New World) tend to misapprehend this character in the long past of the universal church is that we find ourselves a minority in the midst of a society spiritually hostile; we are compelled by that position to a strict discipline: we have no active experience of disunion within living memory. The proportion of regular practising Catholics in comparison to the total body is very high indeed. And at the same time we are not in contact with overt persecution.

Whether this state of affairs will remain, we cannot tell.

At any rate, whether the situation in which we have found ourselves during the last hundred and fifty years or so is destined to endure or not, it accustomed us to strict order within the Catholic body and it has made us regard an equable, peaceful, united Catholic life as normal to Catholic culture.

That the life of the Church was one fierce conflict throughout the first three centuries is a commonplace; but that conflict did not cease with Constantine; it continued in other forms. It continued without ceasing for century after century. Almost exactly coincident with the great movement of conversion about 320-330, whereby people began to come by swarms into the official religion (which had hitherto counted, perhaps, not more than a tenth or an eighth of the whole population), the very nature of the Faith was threatened by the Arian perversion.

It is so remote from us that we do not realise it; and ever since the eighteenth century, especially in England under the influence of Gibbon's essentially unhistorical mind (and Gibbon was but the pupil of Voltaire), it has been the fashion to laugh at the Arian affair as though it were an almost incomprehensible and certainly ridiculous dialectical quarrel; hair-splitting and word-juggling.

It was enormously more than that. It was a whole perverted aspect of the Catholic Church, affecting a great body of the hierarchy, established like a parasite *within* the organism, and threatening to starve and ultimately destroy its life. For Arianism was essentially the rationalising spirit—that is, the inability to see that there are things beyond reason. It was not a whole-hearted rejection of Catholicism, but it was the beginning of one; and in this it closely resembled one side of the Protestant movement in the sixteenth century. It was the spirit that asked of the Mysteries, "How can such things be?"

Now, Arianism lay heavy upon the Church for centuries. It was off and on the Court religion. It became in the main the soldiers' religion in a society wholly dependent on the army; and it was not until three good lifetimes after its inception that a really strong reaction against it began, through the conquests of the army under Clovis over Gaul. The soldiers who governed Spain did not abandon Arianism till later still—nearly a hundred years later. The federate troops which took over North Africa were Arian, and persecuted Catholicism in that province of the Roman Empire as violently as did the Protestant supremacy persecute Catholicism in Ireland. The military power that governed Italy was Arian, and hardly had the Catholic Emperor recovered Italy to his direct rule, when another body of federate troops, the Lombards, also Arian, mastered the North. Arianism had its Bishops, its organisation and propaganda, its powerful effect over the ruling classes (it was happily weak among the poor), for a good three hundred years in one place or another.

The Catholic Church then, though triumphant over paganism after A.D. 300, entered into a new conflict which was not achieved for another three hundred years.

But the date A.D. 600 does not roughly mark the beginning of peace. It only marks the origins of a new battle following the death of Arianism.

Hardly was that peril over when there came the overwhelming heresy which later took on the aspect of a new religion, but which was essentially in its origin a mere simplification of, a degradation of, the Catholic scheme: Mohammedanism. It swept over whole provinces. It conquered Syria, most of Asia Minor, Egypt, North Africa, and at last Spain itself. Wherever its government was established the Christian community dwindled in power and in numbers; in some places the Faith was actually extinguished by its effect spread over a generation; in others a Christian population survived (in Spain a great majority), but subject, and everywhere perhaps somewhat tainted by the infection.

Does Modern Europe appreciate how desperate the Moslem assault was, or what far inroads it made into Christendom? Spain was at last recovered by centuries of hard fighting, but the Inquisition did not get

rid of the last rebellious and secret remnant of Mohammedanism there till after eight hundred years. In
the East Mohammedanism advanced to the capture
of Constantinople within a lifetime of the Reformation. While the Reformation was already in action,
it seized Christian Hungary, and as late as the end
of the seventeenth century, after Dutch William had
ruined Ireland and usurped England, it hung by a
hair whether Vienna itself should not be ruled by
Islam and the Church of St. Stephen become a
mosque; for Vienna was only barely saved by the
gallantry of a Polish king, when Marlborough was
already approaching middle age, when Louis XIV was
growing old, when Newton was publishing his "Principles."

Immediately after this first violent rush of Islam
in the Dark Ages came the assault of a new barbaric
Paganism from the North and East. The pirates out
of Scandinavia did all that such anarchy could to
destroy Christendom; so did a vast eruption of Mon-
gols from Asia. Their vanguard got into the heart
of France. They imposed their language upon the
Hungarian plain, where it is spoken to this day.

It is true that this Pagan attack, being less organised than the Mohammedan, was finally dissolved;
but it had lasting consequences. Scandinavia was not
fully Catholic till seven centuries after the peace of
the Church under Constantine. The great Lithua-
nian duchy was Pagan till nearly the end of the Middle Ages.

Introductory

While our Catholic culture was thus fighting for its life against such mortal and such powerful enemies, the pressure kept unity fairly strict. But when that pressure was relieved internal dissension at once arose, and with the early Middle Ages—from the twelfth century—you have once more within the very heart of Christendom, as formerly in the case of Arianism, the beginnings of what looked like a complete disruption. The plague had begun sporadically, with communities here and there. It took body and strength in what was called the Albigensian movement.

This was a peculiarly vile perversion; Manichean (or, as we say to-day, "Puritan"), and producing a social effect of the worst kind, ruinous to beauty without and goodness within. Yet it rapidly became dominant in the richest and most central part of Catholic Europe, the South of France, during the last half of the twelfth century—that is, in the lifetime before 1200. In the early thirteenth it was spreading everywhere, and it looked as though it might win. It had a very strong organisation of its own: its own bishops and priests and councils: it was only conquered after the most desperate fighting and through the inspiration of St. Dominic; the struggle was like the difficult stamping out of a raging fire. Great parts of Spain sympathised with the Albigensian revolt: a Catalan army of 100,000 men came up in relief of the Albigensians, and had it not been for the battle of Muret in 1213, Catholicism and European civilisation to-day might be confined to some isolated corners of Europe; or perhaps might not have survived at all.

There was a breathing space: the breathing space of the high thirteenth century.

It did seem at last between, say, the years 1220 and 1300, as though a full Catholic society, finally secure, had been established in Europe everywhere. That society was confronted, it is true, by a very powerful Mohammedan foe which had conquered half the Roman land, all Africa, nearer Asia and half Spain. Yet the restricted Christendom of St. Louis, and St. Ferdinand, St. Thomas, Edward I, and the two de Montforts—the Christendom in which had arisen the Universities and the Pointed Arch—seemed settled.

Yet, just after this brief respite, with the first generation of the following century, appeared the first symptoms of a new peril which was graver in effect than any of the former ones: it was the peril of disruption.

The Papacy first became politically a French thing; later was divided between various rival claimants, in what is called the Great Schism. In the midst of that century (1300-1400) there fell upon Catholic Europe the Black Death, from which its political and social constitution never recovered. Obscure but intense spiritual revolts appeared for the first time even in England, though England of all the old Roman provinces had hitherto shown an uninterrupted aversion to heresy, and a peculiar devotion to Catholic

unity.   Later, such revolts broke out with more viru-
lence—because they had language and nation behind
it—among the Bohemians of John Huss.

The conception, then, of the Christian centuries
between the Peace of the Church under Constantine
and the crash of the sixteenth century, as a period of
fixed, easy, united Catholicism is most erroneous.   It
was all peril, all conflict, and all recurring imminence
of disaster; the final catastrophe just barely staved off
time after time, and that only in a part of what had
once been our general European culture: for the
South and Southeast were abandoned to Mohammedanism.   By the end of those many centuries had
already appeared what I called the "Advent of
Disaster."

The new "advent" as here used implies no necessary
sequence of events.   No fatal course made the Reformation inevitable.   But the ground was prepared
by a number of successive political and other acci-
dents, such that, when the next of so many perils
to which the unity of Christendom has been sub-
jected appeared, that peril had a particularly favourable opportunity for developing and for ending in
catastrophe.

There is a strong tendency towards the error of
regarding men in the past as aiming at what we *now*
know to have been the fruit of their actions; though
they themselves could have had no guess at such
results, and though they would have been astonished
and even appalled had they been told what the con-

sequences would be. So it was with the men who began the Reformation.

The Reformation, though the hidden driving power of it lay in the avarice of Princes and other great men, was outwardly and superficially a doctrinal movement. It was outwardly an effort to eradicate certain doctrines (not everywhere nor always the same) from the full Catholic scheme, and to substitute other new doctrines. But the ground for its success was *not* prepared by the comparatively slight doctrinal novelties which had been defended before the general upheaval took place. These had been suppressed, and the memory of them had faded before the main movement arose.

Thus Wycliffe has been called "The Morning Star" of the Reformation as though his particular movement (which had a short-lived but considerable success in one narrow field out of all Europe) had led directly through a chain of further doctrinal innovations to what followed more than one hundred years after his death. With rather more reason, but still erroneously, the much more formidable movement in Bohemia, coming almost exactly a century before Luther's protest, has been made the main origin of the affair.

It was not so. The outstanding character of the process that went on for full two hundred years before the Reformation was not the positive growth of new doctrine but *the weakening of moral authority*

[30]

in the temporal and spiritual organisation of the Church.

After the Catholic triumph of the thirteenth century, the cutting out of the Albigensian cancer, the rise and flourishing of the two new great popular Orders, Franciscan and Dominican, the profound effect of the great Church Councils and the codification of Philosophy and Theology under the supreme genius of St. Thomas, there fell upon the temporal, or political, circumstances of the Church a first misfortune, which was the turning of the Papacy into a local power. It became almost an organ of the French Monarchy, which was the exponent of a now already conscious French Nationalism.

What happened was not exactly a conquest of the Papacy by the French King, but the migration, from a number of causes, of the Pope from Rome, his See and natural habitat, to Avignon upon the Rhone. Avignon was not technically part of the French King's dominions. It lay on the left bank of the Rhone, which river then divided territory feudally subject to the King of Paris from territory by this time very vaguely, but still nominally, subject to the Empire—the titular head of which was in practice a German, though in theory he might be anybody.

For centuries there had been conflict between the Empire, as representing the supreme lay power in Europe, and the Papacy, the admitted supreme Head of all the spiritual life of Europe. The Papacy, after intense efforts and unfortunately at the expense of heavy taxation, which weighed upon all Christendom (but especially heavily upon England), had won. The political power of the Empire was in ruins long before the year 1300, and there was a moment when the Papal power seemed to have, even in the temporal political field, no serious rival.

But an obvious replacer of the old Imperial Supremacy among Christian Princes was present in the intact strength of the Capetian Monarchy in Paris. The Lords of what is now eastern and southeastern France began to look to Paris, and it was the French organisation which, after the fall of the Imperial pretensions, grew to overshadow all the West.

Once the Papacy had established itself at Avignon, the intrigue of the French King and the very force of things led to a succession of French Popes.

Such a state of affairs did not at first affect the general sense of unity in Christendom. For though rival Popes were set up occasionally against the true Pope at Avignon, it was the Pope at Avignon who was naturally looked to by the common sense of Europe as the true successor of St. Peter; which, indeed, he was. But there was something unnatural in the divorce between the actual town of Rome and the Roman See: the Apostolic City and the Apostolic claims. The awful tradition of the old capital of the world and the spiritual monarchy of its Bishop were now exercised permanently from a provincial centre, and that provincial centre was dominated by only one out of many Christian Princes, and that one not even clothed with the name of general authority, with the tradition of the Empire. For while the words "Empire" and "Emperor" still carried to men's minds a vague atmosphere of general authority in temporal things, parallel to the general authority of the Pope in spiritual things, no such authority clung to the mere King of France any more than it did to the King of England or the King of Scotland or the King of Aragon or the King of Castile.

Just when this long and unnatural exile of the Papacy at Avignon had done its work in weakening the full authority of the Holy See, the difficulties of the position were greatly increased by the very effort made to remedy it. St. Catherine of Siena, after the Popes had been in Avignon for the lifetime of a man (1307-1377), brought the Papacy back to Rome.

This salutary revolution was immediately challenged. Against the true Pope in Rome another Pope was elected (by French efforts) for Avignon; and there began what is known in history as the Great Schism of the West. Pope stood against Pope. Different sections of Europe paid allegiance, one to the Pope at Avignon, another to the Pope at Rome. The mere mechanical effect of such divided allegiance was disruptive. The idea of unity remained, of course; men all over Christendom still thought of the Papacy as one supreme office, and took its powers for granted. But it weakened that ideal more and more in men's minds to see the fact before them of two human beings, each claiming possession of the office, each

[33]

with the support of half Europe behind him, and each utterly repudiating the claims of the other.

That impossible situation lasted forty years (1377-1417). Not that an effort was not made to settle it long before the expiration of that period, but it was forty years before the tangle was straightened out and one admitted supreme Head of the Church ruled again in Rome. Meanwhile, the rival Popes were bound to strengthen each his own claim by yielding all manner of privileges and making all manner of concessions to their respective supporters. The old unflinching direct authority, exercisable against kings, which had been the glory and the power of such men as Innocent III, three lifetimes earlier, was gone.

Consider the effect upon men throughout Christendom, not only of the unnatural exile at Avignon (itself accompanied by the occasional setting up of anti-Popes) nor only of the Great Schism, but of the *length of time* involved.

The great changes in human society are strongly affected by the scale of human life. What is beyond living memory ceases to have any very active effect. Now, when the Great Schism began only very old men, too old to impress the world with their moods and traditions, could remember the undivided and unchallenged unity of the Papal See of their childhood. By the time the Great Schism was finally healed the old unquestioned state of European unity under one all-powerful Pope was away back in long-past history. Men who were between thirty and forty when Martin V acceded in 1417 to a Papacy once more fairly united had passed their whole lives in contemplation of the Schism, just as men between thirty and forty to-day have passed the whole of their useful lives under the influences of the twentieth century. On such men the era before motors has left no vivid impression; it belongs to their early childhood. The era before telephones is to them ancient history. They find it difficult to realise it. Even older men who were in late middle age when Martin V was raised to the Papal Chair and the Great Schism ended, were as far away from the beginning of the trouble, the exile at Avignon, as men of my age are from the French Revolution, or as are very old men to-day from the American Declaration of Independence.

But the "sequelæ" of the Schism went on for twenty years after Martin V's accession. There were still attempts at rival Popes till nearly the middle of the fifteenth century.

By the time the Schism had really ended—with the accession of Nicholas V: 6th of March, 1447—the first removal to Avignon was one hundred thirty years away up the stream of time.

In other words, till less than a long lifetime before the Lutheran movement, all Christendom had lived as much under the impression of a divided and increasingly despised Papacy as all our last two generations have lived under the increasingly important

effects of mechanical invention. The Papacy at
Avignon was what steam machinery and communi-
cation are to us. The Great Schism which followed
on it was like what the telephone and the motor-
car are to us. One may say that the prime condition
of Christian unity, a single and powerful headship,
had disappeared.

Two general surveys of Europe in the fifteenth century (1400-1500) have to be made before we can begin to understand how and why that explosion ab-
ruptly followed at the beginning of the sixteenth.
The first is what I would call "the last lifetime"—a
survey of the eighty years or so between the thirties of
the fifteenth century and the initial protest of Luther
in 1517. The second is a survey of that special and
determining point, the condition of the Papacy and
of the Papal court during the same period.

The last lifetime before the Reformation was a
very distinct period over all Europe: the fruit, of
course, of what had preceded it, but something very
different from what had preceded it. We can understand it best by remembering the three names which
attach to it in different degrees of accuracy.

It has been called by the anti-Catholic Germans
"the clearing up," i.e., the dissipation of the mists of
religion—which they regarded as false legend—and
of what they despise as the "mental confusion" of
the Middle Ages.

It has been called "the failure of Christendom," i.e.,
the breakdown of the united Christian civilisation of

the West, wherein even to the end the growing nations had remained provinces of one essentially homogeneous thing.

It has been called the "spring of the Renaissance," i.e., the opening out, the flowering, of a vision—the vision of that high and splendid Pagan antiquity from which we all derive—the vision of Greece and of Rome as they were in their highest culture.

The first of these names, "The Clearing-up," is true or false according as you accept or deny the transcendental doctrines of the Catholic Church, especially the central doctrine of the Incarnation and all that flows from it, down to the last details of local devotions to the Mother of God. There was certainly a prodigious revolution in the European mind, and you may call it, according to your lack of faith or your possession of it, the getting rid of illusion—that is, waking up—or a loss of the sense of reality upon eternal things.

The second title, "The Failure of Christendom," is also true of one aspect of the affair. Europe was ceasing to be united, and it has never been united since. But we ought not to accept the doctrine that the separation of its various parts was bound to proceed increasingly. The centrifugal tendency might well have proved a passing evil. Reaction was bound to come; and, indeed, did come. What is more, a powerful, instinctive counter-tendency for the re-uniting of Europe has appeared again and again since then, and has tried to realise itself; and though it has always hitherto failed, we must not be certain that it will not succeed in the future. I myself have always thought that under the pressure of things too alien and really imperilling our common European tradition, unity would re-arise.

The third title, "The Spring of the Renaissance," is undoubtedly exact. Through causes far too profound and therefore too hidden for us to discover them, causes working in the spiritual depths of man, there passed over the European spirit in the fifteenth century a fresh wind comparable to that which had made the great medieval civilisation four hundred years before, but blowing more strongly, more suddenly, and from a different quarter. It was an air revealing to man the great past of the Mediterranean and filling all the strongest minds of the day with a passion for the recovery, and, as it were, the living over again of the classical past.

It is customary to ascribe this astonishing, vigorous, new aptitude and pulsing of life to material causes, such as the dispersion of ancient manuscripts throughout the West by the advance of the Turks in the East; and notably to the capture of Constantinople in 1453. Such an explanation seems to me grossly insufficient. Pictorial art had been moving towards the new spirit for two generations in the South, the change in architecture had already begun. So had the critical examination of documents, the passion for the discovery and editing of new texts— long before the New Mohammedan pressure upon the East had dispersed manuscripts mechanically throughout the West.

But whatever the causes were, the thing was a mental revolution, and it was under the stress of this revolution that the old-established and apparently secure fabric of the united Catholic world shook, and at last split through a mishandling of the crisis.

New learning, new and much-expanded experience shakes Faith for this reason: that we can only think in pictures, in phantasms of the mind. Our belief that this or that is true is associated with some image within us. Sudden new discoveries disturb this association of true ideas with insufficient images. That disturbance struck Europe in the time of which I speak.

For there went with the great change an expansion of knowledge and a new experience in material things which ran with increasing effect. A man born just before the beginning of the period of which I speak, say in 1430, and living to old age, would have seen before he died the following things: the expansion of geographical knowledge out of all previous conception; the turning of the Cape of Good Hope by the Portuguese, and their discovery of a new way to India; the planting of small garrisons of our race in the islands of the Atlantic, on the coasts of Africa, and of India, and of distant Asia; the increasing realisation of what many men had always known (perhaps most men who thought of such things had vaguely taken it for granted), that the earth was a globe: the bringing forward of a perpetually increasing mass of ancient learning and of loveliness in statuary, in letters, and in building; the beginnings of the art of printing, first obscure, then developed, at last universal; the use of paper which was its concomitant and necessary condition; the flourishing upon every side (after a growth of from one to two hundred years) of vernacular literatures, as in France, Spain, Germany, Italy, and England. It was the moment also of a change in the art of war almost comparable to the great change of our own time, since it became possible for those who possessed the new large artillery—and only national governments could possess this—to dominate absolutely. The last shreds of dead feudalism were swept away; the castles were no longer independent. It is true that this particular change—the change in warfare—was slow to mature, and men hardly grasped its significance until the following century, after 1500; but it was there, present, and some few had already grasped it; notably the Kings of France.

A man born, as I have said, at the opening of this new period—say, about 1430—would, when only just over sixty, have heard of the voyage of Columbus. He might conceivably in extreme old age have heard that a Pole on the frontiers of Christendom had suggested the movement of the earth, though he could not have lived to have seen the printed work of Copernicus.

Meanwhile there would have been going on all

around him the rise of greater and greater vigour in that "humanism" which was produced by the study of antiquity. He would have been filled, as all the most vigorous minds of the day were filled, with an increasing contempt for the medieval past; he might even have felt secure of some glorious future for the human intelligence; indeed the present was for many of them sufficiently glorious in their new-found knowledge.

This great expansion of experience, emotion, and knowledge created in all men's minds a disturbance (though it was in the minds of the most vigorous a pleasant disturbance) which in some of its aspects approached anarchy. The late Lord Salisbury, who said so many true and profound things, remarked some thirty-five years ago upon a parallel effect today, saying that our sudden expansion of knowledge in physical science had shaken popular and traditional standards or morals and was accountable for the modern revolts.

Yet this lifetime before the Reformation did not immediately breed heresy. On the contrary, it was a period in which men were somewhat fatigued of heresy. The Lollard movement in England shrank into insignificance: the Hussite movement in Bohemia shrank into nothing more than a local grievance.

What this new state of mind did produce was a considerable scepticism, which was much more evident in jest and epigram than in definite statement. Antique learning, notably the Grecian, was at issue with the Christian Faith, and a pride in "Humanism" (as it was called) went with a scoffing at legend *and* at dogmatic truth; for the critical examination of legend was proceeding apace and entangled in its fall was doctrine.

That was the lifetime in which, for instance, the Donation of Constantine (which had long been supposed the origin of the Pope's temporal monarchy) and the unauthentic Decretals of Mercator (some of which supported particular developments in the Papal power) were re-examined and increasingly rejected. It was the time in which a huge mass of what was apocryphal or semi-apocryphal in tradition was thoroughly searched out and discredited: too much so, as we now know. For the great scholars of this "Humanism" had no patience even with the truth that lurks in the most fantastic legend. It has required a further advance in learning to teach men that the wildest stories in life of Saint or account of shrine are often based on some real historical event, and are nearly always of service as evidence.

At the same time a new enquiry into the text of Scripture had tardily arisen, and, on the eve of the Reformation, the Hebrew books not only of the Old Testament but of the Talmud, were familiar to many, as were the Jewish arguments against the Faith. As for the Greek Testament, it was the very test of scholarship and known by heart. There was another element of disturbance in that tumultuous time. The Turks had begun their triumphant and disastrous advance towards the West. Garrison by garrison they ate up the Christian control of the Eastern Mediterranean; they streamed over the Balkan peninsula (Albania alone could resist them). Greece went, and when such a witness as I am describing would have been in his twenty-third year, came the crash at Constantinople, the capture of that city by the Turks and the end of the Roman tradition of the Empire, after a continuous life of fifteen hundred years.

Under the pressure of all these forces one effect was lamentably apparent. European morals were for the moment breaking down.

In the midst of such confusion that which should have served to moderate by authority and to reform by example, the Papacy, failed to play its part.

Side by side with the weakening of the Papal authority there went on in Religion during this century and a half between the Black Death and Luther's first protest a process the character of which it is absolutely essential for us to grasp if we are to understand how the Reformation came about. That process is difficult to define because it was subtle, because it did not appear in the names of things (and it is by the names of things that men usually judge), and because it was only felt by contemporaries in the shape of a certain ill-ease of which they did not fully recognise the nature.

I will call that process "A Crystallisation of Religion." By that term I mean a sort of hardening in what had been elastic and fluid, an exaggeration of routine and precise rule as opposed to latitude of movement; a growing of the letter against the spirit; a preponderance of the framework of the living organism, as against the flesh and blood thereof. One might call it "a hardening of the arteries."

The enemies of Catholic truth have used for this process which afflicted the Church during the end of the Middle Ages the term "Fossilisation."

That term, of course, I deliberately reject. It is not only exaggerated, it is false. The life of the Church continued vigorous and holy; she produced great saints; her administration perpetually subserved the needs of man; Europe lived a truly Catholic life and was sane. But what may be called her official life—hardened out of measure. With that there necessarily went a fixity of abuses. Fixity of the good even in that institution which is the supreme hope of mankind we can never have, because the nature of man is fallen; the doctrines, the holiness, the supreme spiritual value of the Catholic Church remain, but its political machinery must be subject to constant renovation. Anything which interferes with a ceaseless attention and readjustment tends to weaken the organism.

Just as the term "Fossilisation" is quite false, so, and still more false, is the term "Old Age." The Middle Ages grew old, but the Church did not grow old. All she suffered from, as the Society in which she lived grew old, were certain constraints of which in due time she rid herself; and never did the life of the Church, even in its human activities, rise to a more splendid vigour than after the final challenge of the Reformation had been delivered and had so nearly succeeded.

As examples of this crystallisation take the complex network of clerical finance. The old simplicity therein disappeared. Dues were exacted on mere precedent, though the causes of such precedent had ceased to be. Burdens which had been necessary when the Church was fighting for its life against the lay power continued, some of them at least, when they were no longer needed. Or take again such abuses as pluralities. In the earlier ages—for instance, in England after the Conquest—for a man to hold even two Sees at once was a thing occasionally done but not tolerated. It was a scandal and an outrage. In the later Middle Ages it became accepted; still denounced and still scandalous, but accepted.

And here I return to a main origin of this breakdown called the Reformation, perhaps the chief root of all, the Black Death.

The Black Death half-way between 1300 and 1400 (1348-50) tore through the living structure of Christendom like some horrible weapon tearing through the living flesh and organism of a man. It killed perhaps one-half, certainly more than a third, of Western Europe in two years. It ruined the old hearty structure of feudalism. It lowered the potential of life everywhere in numbers, in vigour and in productive power. In some places whole monastic communities were wiped out, in others the Bishop and all his Chapter died. To give a particular instance, the University of Oxford, an essentially clerical institution, at the very core of English Ecclesiastical life, sank to a third of its old numbers and there remained. To give another: the Monastery of St. Albans, one of the great typical monastic institutions of the West, sank to, and remained at, half its old numbers. The same was roughly true of most of the great monastic houses throughout Europe. Some, later, received further endowments and greater numbers. But the monastic institution, like all other institutions in Europe, was hit in its vitals, and the effect of the blow was felt for generations.

This visitation lowered the standard of culture among the clergy heavily—especially here in England. That standard had largely recovered, and before the Reformation came there had run through it the new life of revived classical learning. None the less, the effect of the blow was felt here also, and permanently.

At the same time the Black Death emphasised local peculiarities in the different provinces of Christendom, and that after a curious and unexpected fashion.

Before the plague the external unity of Christendom was maintained, not only by common doctrine and its consequent civilisation, but also by a very large governing set of people who might be called in modern terms "Cosmopolitan." Throughout the West, though in different degrees, they intermarried, they met each other continually in the Crusading movements, in the great Councils, even in the wars. One very large body of them—most of what counted in France, and all of what counted in England—had a speech sufficiently general to all for all to use it habitually amongst themselves. A gentleman of Northumberland was in language and accent much more like a gentleman of Bordeaux than an educated Englishman to-day is like an educated American. Even where this ubiquity of upper-class French was not familiar (upon the Rhine and beyond it, in Spain and in Italy) there was a come and go which fused the travelling part of Europe together; and that travelling part meant in those days, not only the gentry but very much more; the officials, the soldiers of fortune, the scholars, a large proportion of the clerics.

Now the Black Death had among a hundred other effects the effect of separating local diction and habit between province and province. All this went side by side with a growth of national feeling. The slow division of a United Europe into separate nations would have happened anyhow, but the Black Death accelerated it. It turned England (within a lifetime after it happened) into a wholly English-speaking country, or at least a country in which only the Court and few of the greater men thought in French. It turned the Slavs of Bohemia into a body much more consciously opposed to the Germans. Everywhere it had this effect of what some to-day call

"Particularism," deepening the lines of cleavage between the various divisions of Christian folk.

Of course, the evil had not gone anything like as
far as it has to-day, when even the common use of
Latin has disappeared. Still, there was already by
1400 a very marked difference between nation and
nation, and that difference continued to grow.

It was largely this new local feeling which bred
the local and minor Ecclesiastical revolts like that of
Wycliffe in England and of Huss in Bohemia.

Lastly, we must note in the midst of all this process
of ill-ease a dissatisfaction with the powers exercised
by the clergy, especially with their very great financial power. Long process of time, coupled with such
revolutions as the Black Death, accentuated by the
diminution of the numbers in the Monasteries and
in Ecclesiastical Corporations, the turning of Ecclesiastical tax and rent-gathering into a routine often
burdensome, in exceptional cases monstrous—all this
affected the mind of Europe with an unceasing
anxiety and disgust.

If the modern reader desire a modern parallel, there
is one immediately to hand. The morals of all of us
(save of a small eccentric clique) admit the rights of
private property. Further, we are all of us (except
a few cranks) attached even to its traditional forms.
We take no great pleasure in seeing great fortunes
ruined; we all think we should combine to prevent
violent economic disturbance in the State. None the

less we are, as a society, full of anxiety and ill-ease when we contemplate modern industrial capitalism. It has its official defenders, but they carry little moral weight. There is a confused but very strong desire for a reform towards greater justice.

Now that is a good modern parallel to the cry of society in the later Middle Ages. The demand for a cleansing of the Church grew louder and louder. It was expressed in a universal formula, "A Reform of Head and Members"; of the head because the scandal of the Papal Schism was becoming intolerable; of the members because of the lay discontent with the forms of revenue accruing to the clergy. To take but one instance out of hundreds, there was bitter and increasing discontent with the often abnormal burial dues, rigidly attached to particular corporations.

Such then was the general process leading up to the last lifetime of a united Christendom—the last half or two-thirds of the fifteenth century. That last lifetime seemed upon the surface a more agreed and united period than the two lifetimes which had preceded it, but under that surface strongly disruptive forces were at work; the Papal Court was turning into an Italian Principate; scepticism was very rapidly spreading; and a sort of moral anarchy was beginning to appear, not in society but within a host of individual minds through the too sudden expansion of the world.

We are now arrived at the period just before the upheaval; the period during which accumulated the forces which produced the great explosion. Since that explosion directed its main effort against the Papacy, let us conclude by considering how that institution stood in the last long lifetime before it was so suddenly challenged.

It is true to say that the condition of the Papacy during the seventy years, 1447 (the election of Nicholas V) to 1517, when Luther published his famous Protest, was one chief cause of the religious upheaval in the West. But what is not true, and what gives a thoroughly false view of history, is to represent that condition as one of nothing but scandal, corruption, and enormity.

The condition of the Papacy a lifetime before the Reformation produced evil effects through sundry factors negative and positive. Negative—that is, not due to the Popes, but arising in spite of the Popes. Positive—that is, due to the action of the Popes themselves. Of these factors, the negative were the more important. Of the positive, that is, of those due to the action of the Popes themselves, the presence of scandal even of occasional excessive scandal, was but one, the true value of which I will estimate later on.

Both parties to the great debate which has proceeded since the beginning of the sixteenth century have from very different reasons tended to exaggerate the evil state of the Papacy at this time. The Catholics who have maintained the traditions of Europe and who have continued to insist that the Papacy is the supreme institution of our civilisation have been shocked, as contemporaries were not shocked, by the Papal Court of the time. The disaster of disunion and of successful revolt brought up the delinquents with a round turn. For centuries we have lived in the atmosphere of a Papacy politically weakened, but morally respected. When we read of Popes who acted after the fashion of civil rulers in their time (even as to their crimes, certainly as to their temporal good qualities), as luxurious princes and international politicians, it clashes with what we both desire the Papacy to be and are proud to say the Papacy has so long been.

On the anti-Catholic side, it is a natural and inevitable tendency to present the many errors, the few crimes, the general falling from a proper standard, which marked the Papal Court and power at this moment, with dramatic emphasis. There is ample material for such emphasis, and the wonder rather is that, especially among modern anti-Catholic historians, we have had such coolness of judgment and restraint in the matter, to atone, perhaps, for the very unhistorical attitude of their predecessors.

What damaged the Papacy and its power in the lifetime before the Reformation was above all this— that it had become an Italian Principate.

It was more secure from violence than ever it had been in all its long history. The Popes were monarchs of Rome and of the Papal States, drawing their great revenues, splendidly enriching their capital and provincial cities with monument and endowment; controlling armies (but local armies) as they had never done before. Yet if ever there was a moment when it would have been to the salvation of Europe that the Papacy should have been general rather than particular, European rather than provincial, this was the moment.

The individual Popes are not much to be blamed in this matter. The thing had come about by the effect of the Great Schism and of the exhaustion following upon it. Perhaps if some man of great vigour and great genius had arisen in that succession between Nicholas V (1447) and Leo X (1513) the old universality would have re-arisen; but no such man appeared.

Let us examine the affair more closely. There are ten Popes in this series, one was a phantom appearing only for twenty-six days—Pius III; there were nine that counted.

Now of these nine we must have a clear conception, free from legend. Nicholas V, first of the undisputed, unpersecuted, and absolute monarchical Popes, was as learned and cultured as he was pious. The next, Calistus III, a Spaniard, was a man full of mortification, full as an individual of the Catholic spirit. (Both of them came to the throne at a mature age, the one at forty and the other as a man of sixty-seven.) Pius II, though marred by a light and irresponsible youth, during which illegitimate children were born to him, came to a sound manhood, and was one of the great scholars of history. (Æneas Sylvius.) He also acceded when his character was ripe and balanced (he was fifty-three years of age) and was rightly respected. He worked hard to unite Europe against the Turkish conquerors. His successor, Paul II, was worldly, but gave no grave moral cause for offence when Pope. His successor again, Sixtus IV, a man of poor origin, cannot be said to have acted in politics other than would any civil prince of the time—but his action was wholly worldly and his reign was the occasion of the first grave scandal—the plot of his nephew, Cardinal Riario, against Florence.

Innocent VIII, who came next, had a worse position through the presence of an illegitimate family—born to him before he had taken Orders, but patronised by him and, as it were, taken for granted. At last, in 1492, when the men who were to be in their maturity at the outbreak of the Reformation were already old enough to receive the lasting impressions of youth, Alexander VI was crowned, and his eleven years (1492-1503) did all manner of harm.

Modern scholarship has toned down somewhat the more monstrous of the legends which once surrounded his name, but modern attempts to excuse him have failed. His career, even had he been but a lay Italian noble of the day, would shock the narrator of it. In a Pope it was tragic. But even here there is much to be remembered on the other side.

Though he was elected through his wealth and

probably through bribery (only by the bare requisite two-thirds majority; by one vote—his own), yet he was politically an excellent candidate. He had been Chancellor administrating the Papal States for thirty-five years; he was a first-rate political governor of the town of Rome. He served commerce by protecting the Jews, of whom he was a sort of patron. He administered justice vigorously. He saw industriously to the details of administration, and all the worst things of his reign were the actions of his abominable illegitimate son, Cæsar, who had no virtue but that of courage.

Others of the Renaissance Popes had children. But Cæsar Borgia had been born when Alexander was a priest, and even a Cardinal. Alexander had no respect for the sanctity of his office. And when one can say that of the Chief Priest of Christendom in a moment when Christendom was in jeopardy, one has said the worst. When all is weighed, Alexander VI was a source of enormous scandal to the Church, and his life and character shook and cracked the edifice of Papal Prestige. He only reigned eleven years. But those eleven years were of lamentable and permanent effect. They are still felt.

He died before the storm broke. His successor, Julius II, a man of sixty, was again no cause of scandal, though a militant determined upon a political programme to be carried out under arms, and to include the freeing of Italy from French influence. He also died before the breaking of the storm. And his successor again, Leo X, also worldly, magnificent, the son of the ruler of Florence, the active inspirer of great art and a man as generous as he was cultured, was certainly of a sort that would have strengthened the Holy See in normal times. He was not a sceptic, as a foolish later legend represented him to be. He was chaste. He had a high idea of his duty in all political things, and a sufficient one of it in spiritual things—but he had no conception of the peril that was right upon him.

Thus, while only one of these nine men was personally impossible, though but three of the nine had lived scandalously in the past, and but four suffered from the scandal of others in their close connection, though the majority were pious, though nearly all were learned, and all without exception active promoters of everything that was increasing civilisation around them—and particularly of the arts—the vital thing about them was that they were, particularly in their own eyes, not so much universal shepherds as Princes of Rome. And with this there went a dynastic spirit of family relationship which is wholly improper to the Hierarchy of the Catholic Church, but which has so often threatened its dignity.

All of these Popes without exception had arrived at their position after an apprenticeship in the intrigue of international and Italian politics, most of them had spent years, the earlier ones in advancing through the conflicting claims of the Great Schism, the latter ones in playing the politician in the affairs of Rome itself.

Paul II was the nephew of Eugenius IV; Alexander VI was the nephew of the well-living and respected Calistus III; Julius II was the nephew of Sixtus IV. All of these Popes, good and bad, regarded their families as lay rulers regard theirs, and those three of them who were burdened before their accession with illegitimate families, Pius II, Innocent VIII, and Alexander VI (the first, however, before taking Orders), gave their families every sort of promotion. All of them were pluralists loaded with the revenues of many Sees and other benefices, while those who advanced their younger relatives did so with the most shameless accumulation of pluralities. Shameless it is to-day in our eyes, and shameless it would have seemed in the older and purer days of the Church—yet did it appear normal enough to the men of that time.

I have spoken of negative forces—that is, forces which the Popes could not control—imperilling the Papacy more than did the positive. The chief of these was their failure, through no fault of their own, to carry out the great task proper to their time as heads of Christendom—the calling out of the military power of Europe against the advancing Turk.

I say it was not their fault that they failed. It was much the biggest thing they had to do and they did it vigorously. Nicholas V urged a crusade with all his might, long before Constantinople had fallen. The Christian princes would not hear him. Calistus III, his successor (the first Borgia, a Spaniard), did the same in his short three years. But no one would act. Pius II, the next in order, sacrificed his life in the affair. Since no lay prince would move, he himself took the leadership of an army; but he died at the setting out in the port of Ancona. Paul II, worldly though he was, acceding though he did as a Papal nephew, spent his seven years still insisting on the Crusade—which none would wage. Sixtus IV kept up the incessant effort. No one heeded him. Innocent VIII, besmirching his position with the advancement of his illegitimate children, was yet ardent in this urging of a Crusade, the most necessary of all his duties.

It was not the fault of the Papacy in its temporary decline and heavy spiritual lapse that the chief external task set to it—the saving of our civilisation from armed attack—was not successful. The failure came from those Christian Princes born into the old age of medieval civilisation, or, rather, born in its death agony. They could not or would not see in what peril we all lay—also they did not care. Later they failed to see the results of their own avarice, when they seized the church lands. Now already they failed to see the results of their own avarice and personal ambition when they refused to combine against the Mohammedan.

It was not until a whole lifetime after the religious revolt in the West had broken out, and in the very turmoil of it, that the Western Mediterranean was barely saved at Lepanto; and the last great Mohammedan stroke against the West, which so nearly put the Danube valley under the Turk and might have brought them to the Rhine, was delivered little more than two hundred years ago.

A huge head of water accumulates with a high tide behind a dyke. Its level is far above the fields on the land side. But such tides have been known before without any catastrophe following. Men are accustomed to their security; they cannot believe that the barrier will give way. Some wanton mischief or some accident opens a random breach in one small spot out of many miles. Suddenly the waters begin to pour in; the earthwork crumbles, there is a cataract, a flood, and general disaster; a whole land drowned.

Such a metaphor applies well enough to the sudden cataclysm of the Reformation. The barrier may be compared to the official organisation of the Church, long weakened within its intimate structure (though that weakness was not observed) through the process which I have called "Crystallisation," and through the narrowing of the Papacy in men's eyes to little more than an Italian dynasty. But in a full survey of all that went to render so formidable the pressure against the defences of civilisation, we must take a larger view. Present with, underlying, informing all the mass of particular elements which threatened unity, were four separate forces, all moving towards their highest point of intensity.

As is often the case in history, the order of importance given to them by a long-distant posterity is very different from the true one. These four elements were the weakening of moral discipline among the clergy; the far greater weakening of moral discipline among the laity—particularly the rich; an increasing popular indignation at the failure of the official church to reform itself; lastly, that permanent hatred of the Catholic faith which is inseparable from the existence of the Church on Earth.

The historian of to-day nearly always puts these four factors the wrong way round. He not only exaggerates, but heavily emphasises, the moral decay in the clergy. He is beginning to allow for—but not sufficiently to allow for—the much stronger effect of the breakdown of morals among the rich laity, particularly upon the point of avarice; and he leaves out altogether—usually because he has no conception of it—that intense force never absent throughout the centuries: hatred of the Bride. I think I should add (though it was and is mainly unconscious) hatred of the Bridegroom—the force which produced Calvary.

The corruption of morals among the clergy went with security and routine. It was not universal, but its toleration was nearly universal, and that was precisely the point of danger. For when an institution is menaced by internal corruption, that corruption need not be widespread, it may even be confined to but a few diseased points. Danger usually lies, as in the case of the human body, not in the presence of the ill, but in its neglect.

If you read contemporary work before, not after,

the loot of the Church (what was said about regulars and seculars by those who were out to rob them in the later days may be dismissed—it is worthless), you will find sufficient proof that the evil was there, and that though it was patchy, it was considerable.

To the men of the time the scandal of pluralities and of extreme worldliness was probably the worst feature. To men of our time the contempt for celibacy, and even for the common rules of sexual morals, seems the worst feature. But both had full effect.

I have emphasised the change in the political character of the Papacy. Of importance was the toleration, not continually, but too often, of irregular living in the very head of the Hierarchy. Successive Popes were not only drawn from the great Italian families, as though the Papacy were a sort of endowment, but nepotism was taken for granted, as we have seen. As we have also seen, men who had lived the debauched lives of their noble class later became Popes. It was a portent that such a life as Alexander's could be led openly. As a prince of the time (and that is how he thought of himself) his relations with women had not been of a worse sort than those of his contemporaries. The sexual morals of him and his kind were far better than those of the rich to-day. But they were disastrous in a Pope.

Much worse was the condition of the wealthy laity, and more particularly, as I have said, in the point of avarice. The whole story of that whole class throughout Europe in this time of active discovery, expansion and glory, was a story of avarice. There was nothing men would not do for the violent and rapid acquisition of wealth. They had not, of course, the *doctrinal* disease of our time; they did not regard their vices as virtues, nor call the rapid grasping of a fortune heroic, as we do. The knowledge of right and wrong in this matter was still sound—but the practice was in ruins.

At the same time civil government was more powerful than ever it had been before; and on the top of that, with the advance of modern things, government was becoming more and more expensive. Every prince was avid. Right to the hand of appetites so eager and so unscrupulous lay the immense wealth of the Church, drawn from rents and dues, many of them unpopular, some detested, and burdening, in the main, the common people. The situation was one irresistibly tempting the wealthy to an attack on Church endowments, though no one saw that the attack was coming.

As for this general widespread indignation against the failure of the clerical body to reform itself, we can only measure it indirectly by its effects *after* it had been let loose: but it was everywhere and it was strong.

But the last factor, the hatred of the Faith, though it was numerically by far the smallest, was so much the most intense, and was in the nature of a leaven which could rapidly infect all society, once it was given play.

We must remember that this hatred has always been present. That it is present to-day most Catholics and all converts know well, though the world outside (the world that writes our official history) does not appreciate the presence of this hatred until it is excited by opposition.

Such hatred is natural and inevitable. All energy polarises, and the Catholic Church is the most powerful source of energy on earth. It provokes an opposite pole. Further, the Church is at issue everywhere with man as he is, restricting him always, and, at some time or other in nearly every man's life, violently at issue with pride, ambition, or desire. Over and above, and more powerful still as a provocative, is the Church's claim to absolute authority and universal moral dominion.

That this force of hatred was confined to comparatively few in Europe *before* the defensive barrier of Church organisation broke down is true; but that it was *potentially* present in a very large number, and might be spread like a fire through whole districts, the event was to prove. Indeed, the most striking mark in the words and deeds that followed the catastrophe is this intense, sometimes insane, passion against The Faith.

If men would only read the originals instead of reading tame modern books about them, and if men would concentrate upon the abominations that were practised upon man and upon the works of man, upon beauty in every form, during that delirium of hate, they would understand. Vituperation once set free to express itself spat at all things Catholic, and particularly the Blessed Sacrament and the Holy Sacrifice of the Mass, as well as at the main Officials of the Church. Long before any reply was provoked the venom had far exceeded anything known before in the extravagances of human controversy. There is no doubt at all of the temper with which you are in touch when you read those curses and insults.

This hatred, I say, was, of all the forces at work, the force which acted at the highest voltage. This force it was which drove the rest, when once the rupture of the bonds which had suppressed it gave it full play.

There, then, was the situation: an overwhelming accumulation of pressure behind the dyke, and a toppling menace of catastrophe. Yet no one saw it. When the first breach did come, it came but in one not very important town, by the action of one not very well-known man, who acted with no intention of producing the effect he did. A trickle at the most was first observed; it became, in rapidly successive leaps, a stream, a torrent, a flood.

Yards, then miles, of the earth wall crumbled away in the swirl of waters, and the sea poured in.

CHAPTER I

The Flood

WITH the first years of the sixteenth century all had long been ready for an uproar. The forces of discontent and indignation pressing upon the defences of Christian Unity and the social order it had created were heaped up to breaking-point—and more. The dyke had but to be breached at one small point and all would collapse.

The final touch might have come here, there or anywhere. It came as a fact in unexpected fashion from one provincial incident taking place in the German state of Saxony.

All the world has heard that the Reformation began with the affixing by Martin Luther of certain protests against Indulgences to a church door in the town of Wittenberg, in Germany, upon the Eve of All Souls', 1517. The anti-Catholic official legend makes that moment the point of departure, and (for once) it is right.

Martin Luther was born in the year of the great Rabelais (1483) to parents of small position, the son of a miner or woodman. He was taught his Latin, he entered an Augustinian monastery under some strong emotion (the causes of which are very variously given) when he was twenty-three. He was ordained a priest two years later.

For some reason which historical research has failed to discover (there is a mass of contradictory myth about it), he visited Rome in 1510 or 1511— that is, during the Pontificate of Julius II. Probably he was sent on some business connected with his monastery, or his Order.

There is no *contemporary* proof that the worldliness of the Roman Court or of clerical society in Rome or the abuses thereof (there were plenty of abuses) roused him to any special indignation or had any special effect upon his mind. Much later he enlarged upon the shocking state of the city and its rulers; but that was part of a position later adopted. He read his own excitements of the subsequent controversy and of the populace who inspired him into an earlier experience which had been commonplace enough. There was nothing to strike him as a novelty. All Europe knew that Rome. Its evils and insufficiencies had long been tolerated.

From Rome, then, he returned with no particular mission against it. He resumed his place at home. He was a striking preacher, a man of exceptional energy (which in these young days of his tended to turn inwards and to grow morbid when it did not grow explosive). Though far from being one of the Humanists, he had sufficient learning, especially in theology. He was given the active direction of his monastery and important work in the University of

Wittenberg. He was already in his thirty-fifth year, a man of some local prominence among the Germans; nothing as yet to what he became, but already a man locally listened to. In such a situation he accidentally started the avalanche.

One of the abuses of the day was the abuse of Indulgences. There were no doctrinal abuses, save in the exaggerations and occasional very unorthodox rhetoric of individual preachers in their favour.

The dogma of the Church was the same thing as it is to-day: the merits of the saints may be applied by her authority to ourselves—not to the remission of sin but of its punishment—on our performing some salutary act.

But there was damnable abuse in practice. For one thing there was abuse in the extent of Indulgences; for another in the perfunctory carelessness as to their object, but more in the uncorrected confusion between the payment of money as an alms, and the payment of money as a purchase—a confusion most natural, and one which should have made the authorities exceptionally careful in their exercise of the practice. So far from showing exceptional care their negligence allowed the gross superstition to take root that relief from the punishment of sin could be purchased. Worse than that no one can read the contemporary evidence without deciding that masses of men had fallen into accepting an indulgence as a remission of sin: an absolution.

Julius II had begun the building of the new St.

Peter's stone embodiment of the later Papacy, climax of monarchic Rome. Among other ways of raising the great sums required for the completion of that splendour was the issue of Indulgences, the condition of which was subscribing to the cost of its building. Leo X, now (1517) on the Throne, continued the system, and a disgraceful last example appeared, for which Albert of Brandenburg, the young Archbishop of Mayence, and Leo himself are to blame in different proportions.

The Archbishop had got badly into debt over a transaction which was indistinguishable from simony. The Papal See, in *its* need for money to build St. Peter's, and Albert, in *his* need for money to pay his debts, struck a bargain for what we should call to-day an "intensive" gathering of money, "a drive" by the granting of Indulgences throughout his jurisdiction. The Papal See and he were to share the proceeds.

I have said that there was abuse in the extent of these Indulgences, in the perfunctory character of them, and in the confusion by which the alms given to obtain this Indulgence were taken for a purchase. There was also abuse in the whole ceremony of the thing. Such pomp was used, such official pressure, and the rest of it, that, to the ordinary man, the thing had something in the nature of a command for getting the money out of him. A great deal of exaggeration also repelled him, as though the Papal document licensing the Indulgences had had the importance of a minor Crusade.

How the Reformation Happened

Against this Indulgence there was very strong feeling throughout Christendom. In Spain, one of the greatest contemporary Churchmen, a man carrying weight with all Europe, the Cardinal Archbishop of Toledo, the head of that Church, forbade the promulgation of this Indulgence within his jurisdiction; nor did he act alone.

Among the Germans this antagonism to the Indulgence was accentuated by two forces which it is very important to remember during all this quarrel. First there was the old traditional friction between the German King, as Roman Emperor, and the Papacy. Secondly, there was the new cause of friction, a lifetime old, that the Pope had become an Italian Prince in the German eyes. No longer was he seen, as in the old medieval days, in His Majesty upon the Rhine or the Danube; no longer was he sufficiently felt to be one with all Christendom, and of German Christendom with the rest.

Things were prepared, therefore, for violent disturbance.

When Martin Luther, acting no doubt sincerely, and in good faith, and speaking for the very large body of those who in different degrees combated a corrupt bargain, struck at the abuse, drew up his ninety-five theses, and affixed them to the door of the church of the Castle in Wittenberg, it was not a novel challenge; it was not an act of war; it was but one of scores of such acts normal to the life of the University. Men would put up theses for discussion, in no way binding themselves to a personal belief in the thing defended, but as an act of intellectual exercise; though in this case, of course, Luther was personally convinced of the position he had taken up.

Luther's using a church door for the purpose was of no special significance either. When a man put forward a thing for debate in this fashion, this particular church door was the door which was always used. In this connection note something else of importance. Of Luther's ninety-five theses, eminent theologians have said that almost every one could be defended, or at any rate argued, without peril to orthodoxy.

But the point was this: Luther's action came at a moment of perilous instability, and a wild enthusiasm seized not only the people of the place, but great bodies of German folk. It was a confused enthusiasm, but its general inspiration was unmistakable. It was a violent reaction against the authority of Rome, and, mixed up with that revolt all manner of other breakings out against all manner of other authority: the beginnings of a grumble which grew to a roar from the poor against the rich; the first incitements among the rich themselves towards the raiding of Church wealth for which they were panting; the first horrors of mere freebooters and brigands calling their companions to the quarry. It was not theological debate which this debater on theology had let loose, it was Revolution: one more in the list of those foaming fits and seizures which fall at intervals upon mankind.

The flood rose, boiled and seethed, and mounted prodigiously. Luther suddenly found himself raised hugely into view, on the crest of a wave, the magnitude of which must have astonished him beyond measure.

All manner of converging forces, as we have seen, had united to produce that seismic tide—Humanism, German racial feeling, the eternal hatred of the faith, the avarice of the local princes and lords and squires, in district after district, the loose living of the clergy, the turning of religion into a mechanical process, the scandal of such men in the hierarchy as the Archbishop of Mayence (the immediate cause of the trouble), the condition of the Papal Court—the old cry, more persistent than ever, of a necessity for "reform in Head and Members" which many of the noblest and all the least balanced souls of Europe had insisted on for more than a hundred years.

Rome heard the news like the noise of a great but distant storm, and at first could make nothing of it. There is ascribed to Leo X, the Pope of the day, a phrase likely enough: that it was a mere quarrel of monks. For the Dominicans had the handling of Indulgences, and the Augustinians (of whom Luther was one) were offended by that favour.

But the real situation was soon grasped. By the next spring—that of 1518—Luther was summoned to Rome. He did not go; but it must be carefully noted that there was here as yet no personal rebellion; there were only pleas that his bad health should excuse him from that journey, and so forth. So far from leading, Luther fell behind in the furious mill race he had unwillingly let loose. He was frightened of it and unprepared for it. Authority took advantage of such hesitation in the man whose name was already used as a label for the new anarchy.

The accumulated irritation throughout the Germanies—including the Swiss Cantons—against the Papal political power and its taxation, coupled with what was already a vague feeling of quasi-national difference, demanded that he should be confronted with his opponents at home. It was not desired that the issue should be determined in a distant court which so many men had begun to feel Italian rather than universal. The Roman Court accepted that situation and was prepared to give a local venue.

So Luther did not go to Rome. He was excused. He was allowed to debate his points with one of the greatest and most learned men of the day, Cajetan, in the Imperial Diet summoned at Augsburg.

There is historical irony in the fact that the Diet summoned for this year 1518 had for its chief object the persuasion of the Emperor and of the Northern Princes to combine in a crusade against that towering menace of Mohammedanism immediately to the East, which, within seven years, was to gain so great a victory and imperil all the West. That was truly the great business of the moment, if men could only have

[71]

seen it; yet, as things have turned out, the Diet summoned at Augsburg is remembered for what then looked like the much lesser business of Luther's disputation. And modern historians perpetuate this false perspective. They half ignore the Mohammedan international factor of the time. It was overwhelming.

It was the Mohammedan pressure and its success which finally crippled the Emperor's waning power over the rest of Germanic cities and lordships, made it impossible for him to act against the dissolution of society, and allowed the break-up of religion to run its full length.

In the disputation at Augsburg Luther was offended. He had not been treated roughly by his opponents, the roughness had been on his side. But things had gone against him, and he had been made to look foolish; he had been cross-examined into denying, for instance, the authority of a General Council —which authority was the trump card to play against the Papacy.

It was a year since the breaking of the storm, but there was as yet not so much as the beginning of a new society. No man then living could dream of a coming final disunion in Christendom.

In the early spring of the next year, 1519, Luther is still protesting his Catholicism, using the most solemn adjurations in a personal letter of his devotion to the Holy See, and his protest, we cannot but believe, was perfectly sincere. But he felt the tide under him, stronger and stronger, and it bore him along.

A Conference arranged at Leipzig later in the year was what finally drifted him off from unity and put his now famous name permanently at the head of the rebellion. He came back from that conference at once embittered against his official enemies and inspired by a feeling of popular triumph; widespread and very vocal support poured in upon him from all sides.

Nor was the support popular alone. It was also, and even more, the support of great bodies in the directing classes; the support of the Humanists, ready to struggle in alliance with any opponent against the restraint of tradition, and what they felt to be the corpse of the Middle Ages poisoning the new life of the Renaissance. It was the support, above all, of the local Princes, and below them, of the swarm of lesser nobles. Luther's own Sovereign, the Elector of Saxony, and a mass of small squires and their cadets, seeing before them independence and the requisition for Church wealth, smelt opportunity for themselves and their fortunes in this still blind, almost universal protest and upheaval against established order as represented by the titles and claims to authority of the Emperor, and by the organisation and endowment of the Church.

It must especially be remarked that in the brief time which had elapsed—not yet twenty-four months —since the origin of the quarrel, the defence of tradition and orthodoxy had been swamped in the turbulence and clamour of the moment. It ought not to have allowed itself to be swamped.

Before the end of 1519 Luther had gone through a revolution within his own mind, and also as to his position. He had become a violent opponent of the whole Church system. He had allied himself for the moment with every form of discontent. He was the hero—and glad to be the hero—of a general insurgence. In the next year, 1520, came the Bull of Excommunication—*Exsurge Domine*—with a delay of sixty days for submission. Of course, no submission was made, and it is from this moment that the advance of the Reformation became patent to the observer, though, as I have said, the original and comparatively insignificant original date is October 31, 1517. Henceforward the attack gathers weight, and the defence begins very tardily to rouse itself. Henceforward also a new, inevitable element appears in the confusion: the element of progressive denial. The loss of faith.

There had already come in to support the principal movement the German Swiss Canton of Zurich. There Zwingli, a priest, hitherto orthodox enough, enjoying a Papal endowment for many months after Luther's first step; a man, unlike Luther, of high position in the world of scholarship; one who had, *with the support of the Archbishop of Constance,* preached against the Indulgence, came out very much more clearly and logically than Luther had done as a *doctrinal* revolutionary. He procured what was the first official recognition of new *doctrines*. Luther had not as yet seriously or definitely abandoned main doctrines. This new move about to come from Zwingli—with a clearer head than Luther's—was at once affiliated with the Lutheran surge by a common resistance to traditional authority. Of course, Zwingli, like Luther, was no creator of his movement. He was but a symptom, a mark of a universal protest and outburst; not a leader. But the thoroughness of his followers is significant.

The Government of the Canton seized the Church property and decreed the power of priests to marry. It was in 1522 that Zwingli had laid down the principle that the Bible, under private interpretation, was the sole authority for doctrine. He denied the mystery of the Eucharist. By 1525 the Mass had been stamped out in Zurich and its departure had been preceded by a violent iconoclasm committed by these Mountaineers upon all the inheritance of beauty which their ancestors had left them for a guide. Such loveliness was connected with the official Church, and it must go. This was the first of the barbaric destructions. A host of others were to follow through more than a century, ruining the legacy of Scotland, horribly maiming that of France and the Rhine and the Netherlands: murdering our ancestral wealth in living stone.

What followed throughout the whole of Germany, with all its unorganised, dissociated mass of little local lordships, independent and half-independent cities, vague Imperial power over all, was most like that to which I have compared it: a formless, violent torrent of water, such as pours over a broken dam.

The three main characters of the Flood throughout the Germanies immediately after the breaking down of the dam were these:

First, the point made on an earlier page, that the motive power was in essence anti-clerical. A force impersonal, a mob directed from very different sources (small nobles and great, common folk, clerically-over-taxed burgesses, many discontented monks and priests ill-fitted to their vows), all ran in force against the organism of a *clergy;* with the Papacy as the head and symbol of a *clergy;* that is, an order distinct within Society: privileged, wealthy, and possessing sacramental powers.

Everything that happens in the early Lutheran movement turns upon this reaction against *clerical* power. Doctrines and customs of all kinds connected only by the common link that they stand for clerical power: confession, consecration, endowments, alms, and with them "Good deeds"—especially alms for the dead, which the clergy can transfer in a peculiarly valuable way by Masses.

Whatever ritual or doctrine is spared by the Reformers (the doctrines of the Incarnation and Redemption, common prayer in churches, Immortality, the mere practice of a Eucharist, shorn of sacramental quality, the authority of Scripture) is spared because it has this common mark: that a laity may continue to perform such practices, to hold such doctrines without retaining a Priesthood.

The movement was not rationalist. To the Rationalist the idea of an obscure Syrian peasant being the Almighty Creator of all things is far more absurd than any mysterious rite can be. Yet the Godhead of Christ remained, for those myriads in revolt, unquestioned.

The Catholic doctrines retained—especially the root doctrine of the Incarnation—were also to disappear in their turn, as we know. To-day, outside the Catholic Church, their hold on modern men is negligible; but the men of that time had no idea of losing them, as yet. What they desired to get rid of was the Sacerdotal claim; and they were in a passion against it through Sacerdotal abuse.

The second point to seize is a consequence of the first, that this huge chaotic flood was not in its origin what earlier heresies had been, a doctrinal attack upon Catholicism. That arrived later. An opposing religious system was to arrive, with Calvin for its author, set up against the Catholic religious system. But in the first Lutheran movement that new counter-church of Protestantism was yet to come. It did not come till there shone over the universal scene of religious chaos in Europe the cold and clear light lit by Calvin.

The Reformation did not originate in a definite heresy, nor a new, nor a supposedly purified, body of faith. Having arisen as an attack on Priesthood, and the Papal See, through anger against abuses in the Priesthood and the Papal See, it kept this negative and formless character through all its first twenty years. Individuals speculated on doctrine and drew up this formula and that: but the spirit of the great affair was not for making a new organism. It was for wrestling with the old.

The third main point to seize is that the Flood, being a mere flood, impersonal (though released by the activities of some few persons, notably Luther and Zwingli), could construct nothing. It would have effected nothing save destruction; which in its turn would normally have been repaired, had authority had a chance to reassert itself. To continue the metaphor of a flood: the waters would have subsided, tillage and order would have recovered their normal powers—had it not been that political authority over the Germans, already badly weakened and divided, suffered sudden menace in the very thick of the business *from the great Mohammedan victory on Mohács Field*. This left the Emperor a local sovereign fighting for his own hand and unable to reimpose order in Church or State.

In our histories of the Reformation these three main characters—especially the last—are commonly obscured. Men to-day think in terms of what they know was to come, they are interested in the origins of what became a religious civil war throughout Christendom. Because Mohammedanism is no longer a peril they forget that the Mohammedan pressure was in the very years of the first violent quarrels within the religion of Europe, and the crying necessity in those years for that last Crusade which was never undertaken. In other words, our modern official historians make of the first violent commotion in the Germanies, something creative—which it was not; independent and externally caused, which it certainly was not; and affiliated to the later thing called *Protestantism,* which we now enjoy and of which the men of the time knew nothing and (had they known it) would have abhorred. Our historians are wrong: that commotion was at first no more than a hubbub. What made it later lead to a final disruption of Europe was not any force in itself, but first Islam right upon us, and, later, the folly of the Government in England. What gave it later the spirit called "Protestantism" was John Calvin's book.

Let us see why this great Mohammedan victory of Mohács Field and the subsequent advance of the Sultan into the centre of Europe was of such effect in guaranteeing the early successes of the Reformation.

The condition of German society in the early sixteenth century lent itself to a break-up of order and authority upon every side. That hatred of clerical abuse, that reaction against the increasingly local character of the Papal Court, that traditional demand for "Reform in Head and Members," that exasperated misery of the peasants, and, above all, that hunger for loot which anarchy could certainly satisfy, all these produced in the German-speaking centre of Europe at this moment such a field for revolution as was not elsewhere known at the time, nor has been anywhere since.

At the same time the Germans had no true central Government. There was no national German organisation. There was no working machinery for raising an official State army to preserve the general order.

When the Revolt broke out in 1517, the proper organ both for suppressing it and for suppressing its causes—the abuses which had led to the revolt—was the Empire. The Emperor was nominally King of the Germans. But the Princes, that is, the great local semi-Sovereigns, were too strong for the nominal power of the Emperor. The free cities were independent states; the chief bishoprics and archbishoprics were not only ecclesiastical offices but territorial powers equally independent; the whole German-speaking land was a tessellated pavement of lordships large and small. Over and above that, all society was swarming with the small gentry, the families among a village and its serfs, the younger disendowed branches of these families, most of them impoverished, all rapacious, none working: all ready to seize every opportunity for filling their pockets in any fashion that served, and oppressing grossly the masses of the people.

The various steps of Luther's personal career (which is, as a rule, dramatically exaggerated), were but functions of all this social turmoil. Thus, what has been made so much of, his vagary on "Justification by Faith alone," had in its origins no life in it, save that it went with, and proceeded from, a denial of priestly power. It was an afterthought. It was not a motive of the movement. I know that such a judgment is neither popular nor common, but it is true.[1]

The three famous treatises in which Luther broke completely away from the Church grew their strength not from Luther's vigorous pen, so much as from the audience which stood ready, open-mouthed, to swallow them. He defends the marriage of the clergy and the wholly new doctrine that even divorce might in some rare cases be lawful. He does not by this awake a new spirit in men. He only responds to their appetites, and is met with a roar of agreement. His "Appeal to the Christian nobility" is not a blast which stirs to action the myriads of wolfish minor squires, it merely echoes their already aroused determination to loot religion. The Bull of Excommunication launched against Luther is inoperative, not because Luther enjoys some wonderful personal power which magically fends off legal execution; but because the official head of German society is become too weak to follow up at the decree.

But in spite of the weakness apparent in that phantom central German power, that ghost of a German

[1] The Anecdote of the Scala Santa has little historical value, and, anyhow, in no way affected the first movement.

executive, which still called itself the Emperor, the sheer necessity for preserving society and all the inheritance of the past would have reinvigorated the crown had not the fatal day of Mohács intervened. For the Emperor as an individual drew his revenue and such real strength as he had from his own Archduchy of Austria, the patrimony of the Hapsburgs. It was to the borders of Austria that Mohács brought the Mohammedans. It was to a siege of the very capital of Austria, Vienna, that Mohács inevitably led.

At first, even before Mohács, the action of the Imperial power was delayed by circumstance.

The Revolt was only in its first stages when the Emperor Maximilian died (in January, 1519). He was succeeded, after some long delay of intrigue, by his grandson, the young Burgundian King of Spain, known to history as Charles V. When Charles, after being crowned emperor in 1520, had summoned his first Imperial Diet at Worms in 1521, whither Luther was summoned, the scene was not that we are commonly told of a Luther, a popular hero, defying tyranny. It was that of a Government deprived of all real power anxious for German support of every kind and at the same time eager for cards to play against the Papacy, and therefore impotent against a large anarchic movement which was also anti-papal. When Luther was given safeguard, carried away by a ruse of the Elector of Saxony, and hidden in one of his patron's castles, it was not a bold defiance of unjust spiritual pretensions; it was a facile trick, contemptuous of an authority still impotent to act.

Later, as the reaction grew, as the fear of anarchy would stir men to reassert order, as the experience of what anarchy means in practice would rally to authority and tradition the best of the various elements that had been in revolt—especially the scholarly humanists—the Emperor would have gathered forces, his shadowy central power would have gained strength and the order of German society would have been restored.

The Reaction was provided with a strong motive. During the first wild clamour against authority, there broke out two great anarchic movements, side by side: the loot of Church property, of shrines, of all that could be looted, by the gentry, large and small, from mere robbers like Sickingen to great princes like the Elector of Saxony; and a huge rising of the miserably oppressed peasants against the host of lesser and greater gentry into which Germany has dissolved. The peasants' revolt was sporadic, random, abominably violent, murderous, and full of all the very simple doctrines whereby men hope to restore justice on earth through the destruction of all privilege— that is, the destruction of all framework, and therefore the destruction of society.

The peasantry were crushed in vast massacres, mainly by artillery and to the loud applause of Luther himself. The theft of religious wealth by the gentry was more serious—but it might have been halted. The worst of the brief welter was over (it was not yet nine years since the beginning of the upheaval), the muddy waters had begun to subside, when another Imperial Diet (the word means Imperial Assembly) was called at Spires early in 1526. At first it showed what power the movement still had; the Princes, by a majority, decided for the marriage of the clergy, for the relaxing of clerical discipline, and though as yet they put forward no substantial attack on doctrine, they shook the structure of the Church.

But Ferdinand, Charles V's brother, presiding, did what he could to stop the rot. He adjourned that Imperial Conference. The forces already beginning to react in defence of unity were ready to gather, the counter-attack might have begun, when in that same summer, upon the 28th of August, 1526, came this decisive catastrophe of Mohács Field.

Solyman the Magnificent, the young conqueror of thirty-two, who had just driven our Christian garrisons from the Greek sea, marched from Constantinople with 100,000 men and 300 guns. On the wide-open plain, three miles south and west of the country town of Mohács, on the Danube, rather more than 100 miles below Budapest, he met the poor young King Louis of Hungary, with a force of Hungarian gentlemen not a quarter of his own, and killed them nearly all. The Mohammedan on that day destroyed the Christian power of Hungary, the bastion of our civilisation against his attack. He was a conqueror

upon the very borders of Germany, and was henceforward planted at the gates of Western Europe.

The Turks, after Mohács, did not rule from Budapest: they tolerated a native Hungarian king. Austria itself, Vienna, the walled city of the Hapsburgs
(the Emperors), was not immediately attacked after
Mohács. Solyman returned—driving 100,000 Christian captives before him—to his own place. But
Mohács made the Archduke of Austria, Charles V's
brother, Ferdinand, and all that dynasty, feel a sword
hanging over their heads. They must look to their
house as best they could; their power to order Germany as a whole, to rally it against the new religious
disturbance, to restore order and to send the beginnings of the Reformation at once down the way that
all other dissensions against Christendom had gone—
that power had manifestly disappeared.

Mohács made the Hapsburgs *realise* what they
ought long to have known—that Solyman had better
material and a better military machine in recruit-
ment, morale, and methods than anything they could
oppose to him. The Turk of that day was the superior of Europe—yes, even the Europe of the Renaissance—in men and guns and missiles, siege-work and
attack. He had larger, better and more numerous
artillery. He introduced the shell. He may almost
be said to have invented the thought-out scheme of
siege by trench-work, which dominated all our history for more than three hundred years.

It was a close thing whether Islam should not at

last advance to the Rhine. This was the shadow over Europe, and Mohács was its manifestation.

The effect of Mohács upon the new religious chaos in Germany was strong. The adjourned Diet of Spires met in the third year after that military disaster to Christendom. It had sobered men. There was now a large majority for the return to order and unity, but—and this is a significant point—those who refused to accept the decision could not be repressed. The Imperial power no longer had the strength to restrain them. That minority could freely protest with success, and did so. It is from the "protest" of the minority who thus stood out unmolested that the word "Protestant" is descended. That schism was but just achieved, the two main sections, Lutheran and Zwinglian, were at the height of their wrangle, when, that same autumn, the Turk struck a second and more furious blow: he burst into German-speaking land and laid siege to Vienna itself in 1529.

The high value of its garrison, a campaign begun too late, a very early winter, raised the siege of the city; though Islam ravaged the German land far and wide and the Turkish outriders reached the Ems. But the saving of Germany at Vienna owes no thanks to the Reformers. They—the more lucid of them— welcomed the Mohammedan power. Luther himself indeed had the generosity to protest, but the powerful Prince Philip of Hesse more typically showed the spirit of those who had seceded at Spires. He, full of church loot, rejoiced at the Turks breaking into our house. He knew that his own cause was at issue with all the traditions of Europe.

Of the many places in Europe where one can call up the past and the turning-points in the story of our race, one which often returns to my mind—for I have a vivid recollection of it—is the quiet main street of Spires. The noble mass of the Cathedral and its vulgar modern front were before me, the fine town gate at my side, and, opposite the place where I stood, that little eating house which stands upon the site of, and is, perhaps, in part the same structure as the hostelry to which the minority retired and affirmed their "protest"—cleaving Europe.

Dissension has left the place to-day. It is among the most peaceful in the world and among the most happy. Yet here was decided the cause of more dissension in Europe, war more prolonged, and greater unhappiness than any other our race has known.

So ended the first phase of the Reformation: it was still but a violent turmoil, and a turmoil mainly of the Germanies, when a second powerful reinforcement arrived: the political accident whereby England, wealthy, highly organised and under strong central rule, the country which had hitherto least felt the recent storm and was by temper least fitted to abandon tradition, was cut off from Europe.

CHAPTER II

The English Accident

I CALL this, the most important division of my subject, the English *Accident*. I have chosen the word with care.

If ever there were, in all History, an event not desired by its agents; not understood by those who suffered it; coming by no design, but as the prodigious effect of comparatively small and quite incongruous causes, it was the gradual, mechanical and disastrous destruction in the English mind of that Faith which had made England.

Most histories written in the English language represent the English movement as something at once national and inevitable—something that the English nation desired and necessarily in due course achieved. At the same time, while giving in different degrees some hint of the European background, they centre the Reformation upon the English story.

The first of these characteristics, the treating of what happened here as national and inevitable, is historically nonsense. The second is historically sound, though England was but a small nation, yet the blunder of the English Government in separating from European Unity *was* of capital effect in the success of the Reformation.

[88]

The English Accident

There was no national movement against the Catholic Church in England: the little that happened at first was a government movement, and not even a doctrinal movement. It was a mere political and even personal act. What followed it was not a normal process generally desired by the people. It was an artificial process managed by a very few interested men, and these acting not on a religious fad, but for money; what is more, it was a process which, in its first beginnings, gave even these few actors no conception of what was ultimately to come of their greed and folly.

But the concentration upon the English Reformation as being of special importance is, oddly enough, and in spite of the intentions of the official legend in our anti-Catholic academic textbooks, true history.

This concentration upon the English story of the Reformation has indeed hidden from the great run of our educated men the general nature of the Reformation, and especially (what I shall come to later) two main points: that Holland was the example, and that France was the battle-ground. But it is certain that if England had not left the unity of Christendom, that unity would be fully recovered to-day—and long before to-day.

Until England was cut off from that unity of which the Papacy is the living principle, the trouble had stirred in a confused but violent fashion throughout the Germanies and little affected the rest of Europe. Even in the Germanies it had not principally affected the strongest, oldest, and most civilised body of Germans; it had principally affected those sections of the German people who were either cut off by remote mountain living or by distance from the centres of civilisation. It had less deeply involved those Germans who had been originally civilised by the Roman culture.

The statement is general only. Exceptions swarm. Thus Strasbourg, a Roman City (if ever there was one!), counted among those that cut themselves off by the "Protest" at Spires.

But, whatever might happen in the Germanies, and especially in the less civilised Germanies, in England it was otherwise.

England was an ancient province of the Roman Empire, with Christian traditions twice as old as, and far stronger than, those Northern districts of Germany which the Gallic armies of Charlemagne and his successors had compelled by conquest to accept Christian doctrine and practice and to abandon barbarism. Had the English Government not moved, the reaction for Unity, when it came, would have been overwhelming. In a word, it was the separation of England from the unity of the Church, which was, amidst a host of other factors, greater and less, the chief factor in the final event of our disruption. It was the artificial removal of the English from the main body of Europe which made the break-up of Christendom permanent.

It therefore is no exaggeration due to patriotic

bias, or to local distortion of perspective, which makes any sound historian insist upon the capital importance of the Reformation in England. Though no one with historical sense can pretend that the English desired that ruin of their traditions.

Moreover, the English Movement was the first great *official*, or Government, Movement away from unity. The nominal head of the German States had stood firm for the Faith; the more important of the minor German sovereigns had stood firm. Scotland was so far well secured; equally well secured (so far) were the great and dominating French Monarchy, the already united Spanish Monarchy, and the various Italian States. But for the gradual and half-blind destruction of the Faith in England, what we now call the Reformation would to-day appear in history as no more than one of the many outbreaks against the necessary discipline of our culture: a spiritual dissension gradually confined to but one district of Christendom, and that among the least important: Northern Germany with its lordlings. At last the anomaly would have been brought to an end by the pressure of all the rest of Europe.

As it was, the Reformation has come to mean in history the establishment of a new warped culture, the Protestant culture, side by side with the old traditional right culture of our blood: a new culture which quite recently has appeared as the wealthiest, though the most unhappy, of modern times, and might (until the great war) regard itself as the leader of Europe, with Prussia and Britain for its two great poles of energy during the nineteenth century.

How, then, did the Reformation in England originate, and how was it confirmed and made enduring? That is the question I shall attempt to answer.

As we all know, nothing has been more violently debated. There are thousands of books, many of high erudition, written round the point, and any general sketch will necessarily be subject from one quarter and another to strong criticism. Yet I do think the main lines can be drawn clearly and firmly enough. I think the true causes and the true motives can be set down as they were. I shall attempt to do so, although such truth clashes with strong popular preconceptions.

First, as to motive. I have called the very first act—Henry VIII's breach with the Papacy—an *accident*, because I think that word the closest to the truth. An accident—for instance, the side-slip of a motor-car—is not intentional of its effect. It is due to miscalculation upon the part of the driver who, attempting one thing, does another. The miscalculation can often be redressed and its consequences eliminated. It is not desired by him.

We to-day, after centuries of experience in the effects of disunion, take it as a matter of course that an obvious and necessary gulf lies between those who accept the full authority of the Holy See and those who refuse or deny it. In the modern world there is such a gulf. But in the early sixteenth century there was not. To challenge the political power of the Holy See and to refuse to follow its policy, even to forbid for a space the entry of its writs, was a thing that had happened over and over again in the course not only of English history, but of every other national history. The breach had always in the course of time been healed; it had involved nothing doctrinal, that is, nothing offending those religious ideas which had made Christendom: the dogmas upon which were founded the Sacraments, the Mass, the recognition of Orders, and the whole daily habit of Christian folk.

To the Englishman in the street a clash with the Papacy was essentially a *political* clash. That it might breed irreparable evils only some rare wise man could see: as Fisher and More saw. For unity is vital, and Peter and the Church are one. Separation from the Papacy, even temporarily, is not only a denial of unity in the Church, but is an act potent for incalculable evil. But the thing to seize is that such was not the aspect of the affair in the eyes of the ordinary man living in England then, or (for that matter) in any other part of Christendom in the late twenties and early thirties of the sixteenth century.

The supremacy of the King in everything which counted in a man's daily life was a thing not only taken for granted, but of actual and continual exercise. Ever since Edward the Third, the King had appointed without challenge to the great Abbacies and Bishoprics. Statutes administered by the Crown, notably *Præmunire,* showed how far the local power would insist upon its independence against the Papal power in temporal affairs. As for the cutting off of appeals to Rome, why the ordinary man did not carry appeals to Rome! The ordinary man thought of the Pope, of course, as the necessary and unquestioned spiritual Head of Christendom. But the Act admitting a clash in the relations between the very present and powerful and universally accepted Head of the English State and the centre of spiritual authority at Rome, was not an Act shocking, nor even revolutionary, to the plain citizens of that day.

It is very difficult indeed to draw an historical parallel from the modern times for this matter, and the one which I am about to present is not a close parallel, but it must serve.

A body of men within the State to-day refuse to accept a particular law; they resist; the thing has happened over and over again. It is exceptional among us, but not abnormal. They resist an hygienic law, for instance, or a conscription law, or what not. They do not in their heart of hearts refuse the authority of the State; they do not regard their action as one which will have permanent consequences. They act by way of bringing pressure. There lies at the back of everybody's mind a vague conviction, drawn from past experience, that the trouble will blow over; either the State will give way somewhat, or the protesting body will retire of its own accord; or the action will change somehow or other. The old im-memorial equilibrium will return.

Now, it is possible to imagine resistance of this kind (like that of our Conscientious Objectors) leading to consequences more permanent than they had dreamed of, and of a sort which would have ap-palled the originators of the affair. One thing might lead to another till the growth of the movement ended in breaking up society.

I repeat (and I emphasise my repetition), the parallel is a very imperfect one. When Henry VIII broke with Rome, it was on the persuasion of a man, Thomas Cromwell, who was utterly indif-ferent to any consequences so long as he filled his pockets. It was in imitation of certain of the Ger-man under-lords, semi-sovereigns, who had refused the authority of Rome entirely for some years.

Henry's folly was committed at a time when many up and down Europe were clamouring that Papal authority was corrupt and a thing to be challenged. Also, the deliberate rejection of such a bond as that which joined the English Church to the Roman See was far larger in scale and more definite in character than the eccentric modern movements which I have been quoting.

Nevertheless, the main truth stands: the breach with Rome might have been healed, and probably would have been healed, had it remained an isolated act. It was not undertaken out of hatred for the Papal authority, still less out of any doctrinal motive.

How the Reformation Happened

The English people were normal Catholic people of the time. The humanists among them, and also the ardent supporters of reforming abuses, were a powerful group in the Universities and among the bishops; the complainants against clerical dues and exactions were very numerous, one might say universal, and especially strong in London which has always had most to say in English destinies. The irritation against Papal taxation was of a very long standing in England. There was a great deal of irritation against clerical revenue-gathering; especially against church endowments and rents, often payable to distant and decayed houses. But propagators of the new anti-Catholic *doctrines* were here a very small and very unpopular minority, which had as yet had hardly any general effect.

There was a great deal of slackness and indifference, of course, as there nearly always is in an old Catholic society not yet awake to peril. But Henry himself was profoundly Catholic in temper and in faith. He had a special devotion to the Blessed Sacrament, and one only less in degree to Our Blessed Lady; his whole tone of mind was not only Catholic, but, if I may use the expression, somewhat irritably Catholic. The new criticisms of Catholic doctrine shocked and exasperated him, and in the mouths of any of his subjects angered him exceedingly.

How then did so apparently impossible a process as the Decatholicising of Catholic England take place? How did the unexpected, undesigned, and (to that

generation) incredible transformation of a whole unwilling people come about?

It came about thus:—

Henry's wife, Catherine, the daughter of the King
of Aragon, could have no more children. She had
been with child a great number of times, had had
several miscarriages, and had had the misfortune to
lose infants immediately after they were born. There
remained only the Princess Mary; Henry had no
direct male heir.

Now, to have a male heir, if possible, was very important to Henry. We must remember that the
Tudor family was of low origin, it had no real title to
the throne, and in 1525, when the trouble first began,
it was only forty years since it had usurped the throne
of England and replaced the national Plantagenet
dynasty after the battle of Bosworth. The King,
then, gravely needed an heir.

Meanwhile his Ministers, notably the great Wolsey,
were inclined to foster the idea of a new marriage for
the King, in order to support certain schemes of
foreign policy. This new marriage, could, of course,
only be arranged after annulment of the old one with
Catherine of Aragon. But here, again, the modern
reader must be warned against misunderstanding the
past.

"Annulment" did not, and does not, mean that an
existing marriage is dissolved. *It is a declaration that
the marriage was null and void from the beginning:*
that it never had been a true marriage, either because

the parties had not lived together, or because there had not been free consent, or because the husband was related to the wife in a prohibited degree of consanguinity or affinity, or for any other valid reason.

Annulments of marriages (in this sense) where great interests were concerned, were not unfamiliar political and social events. There were continual grants of such annulments by the Court of Rome, whether for the proximity of the parties in blood or from some other cause; the whole of late medieval history is full of the thing.

Henry's own sister had enjoyed (if I may use that term) such annulments. The process was facile: if one party brought the claims and proofs forward and the other party did not oppose them, the thing often went through automatically. If there was a dispute, yet, with anything of a case (as there nearly always was in the tangled relations of the great) the thing also went through, as a rule. The method was gravely abused, but, as often as not, there was a really good case made out, and annulment was granted as it would be quite rightly and reasonably granted to-day; as it is, indeed, granted to-day, to the great scandal of muddle-headed people who cannot follow the perfectly clear principles of Canon Law.

The idea, therefore, of getting the King's marriage with Catherine of Aragon annulled and his making a new alliance had nothing very abnormal about it in the eyes of the time.

Who first suggested the policy we shall perhaps

never know with absolute certitude. There are witnesses who assert that it was Wolsey; others that it originated in Henry; Henry himself said that a French envoy had prompted him, though he puts the story in such a manifestly hypocritical way that it is very doubtful. The best witness of all (because he was in the heart of Court Society), Pole, says that the suggestion first came from Anne Boleyn herself. Anyhow, the idea was there; and Wolsey, as I have said, obviously meant to use it for political purposes and to arrange an important new foreign marriage for the King.

Now Henry wanted to start a love affair with a young and attractive lady about the Court, who counted as a Howard—that is, as a member of the principal family of the Kingdom, semi-royalties, representing the line of Thomas of Brotherton: younger son of Edward I. Her name was Anne, her highly connected but less important father was Boleyn, or Bullen, but her social position and what made her count was that she was a Howard through her mother —for her mother was sister to the Duke of Norfolk. Here let an essential point be emphasised and firmly grasped. It was *not* the mere passion of Henry for this woman, Anne Boleyn, which was the cause of what followed. *The cause of what followed was Anne Boleyn's refusal to yield to Henry and her determination to be Queen.* Anne in her strength was the authoress of what was to come; not Henry, in his inexcusable weakness, the author.

How the Reformation Happened

Henry was not at his first love affair, like the run of Renaissance princes—including many clerical princes—he was a loose liver. He had already had for one of his mistresses Anne Boleyn's own elder sister, whom he had married off rather disdainfully, and with shabby presents, to a minor gentleman. To put it bluntly, he was attracted by the physical type: and he wanted Anne to take her sister's place as his mistress. But Anne's self-control was as strong as Henry's was flabby: she refused to be his mistress, she insisted upon being his wife.

In this condition of desire and balk, Henry quite lost his balance. He was at the young woman's mercy; and at some moment which we cannot exactly determine, but some time in or after 1525, he became so infatuated that he actually proposed to himself the mad idea—for it was mad—of marrying her. I should be inclined to put the date earlier than most people and say 1525; but at any rate it was not later than the beginning of 1527. We can imagine the horror of those who were intriguing for the annulment with international objects, and especially of Wolsey, at such a ruin of their plans! The only possible political good of such a marriage would be the problematical issue of a male heir. High-born though Anne was, the marriage would be a disgraceful one for the King; and it would be the ruin of Wolsey's foreign policy, which hinged on a French alliance to be cemented by Henry's taking to wife a French Princess.

The English Accident

But, of course, Anne's determination to be Queen, which was the driving power of the whole affair, did not come out on the surface; all that appeared before the world was the proceeding for the annulment in the Papal court.

Henry's case was two-fold: first, that Catherine had been really the wife of his boy brother Arthur, who had died in youth. It is true that the young people had been publicly married, but this part of his case was certainly a lie; the children (for they were little more) had never lived together. Secondly (what is theologically unsound), it was in that day widely treated as an open question whether the dispensatory power of the Pope, *if indeed Catherine had really been the wife of Arthur,* did or did not extend to the grave case of marrying a deceased brother's wife, and that therefore the dispensation (which had certainly been obtained by Henry VII for his second son's marriage with Catherine) was of no effect, as being against the Law of God.

When the case came on, Catherine stood absolutely firm against all efforts to make her compromise. She affirmed in the strongest way that her marriage to Arthur had never been consummated, so that the question of dispensation could not arise. She was Henry's wife, and never had been any other man's; and Henry's wife and Queen she would remain.

And here we have a further point upon what is as important to be clear, as it is important for us to be clear upon the way in which people looked upon a breach with the Papacy as only a *political*, not a religious, act, and upon the fact that it was *not* Henry's passion for Anne Boleyn in itself, but Anne Boleyn's tenacious determination to become Queen, which produced the result.

This further point is as follows:—

Had Catherine compromised, I believe that Henry would have obtained his annulment. It is mere hypothesis, and therefore cannot be proved. It is not true, as has too often been stated, that the Pope refused Henry's plea because it was one for divorce (which the Catholic Church does not admit); nor is it true, as has been stated on the other side, that the Pope opposed Henry's plea because he had come under the terror of the Emperor whose troops had captured Rome and who was Catherine's nephew. There were a great many factors at work, as there are in all political problems, but the main point to seize is that the main, the pivot, was Catherine's rigid determination not to be humiliated; her high Castilian honour. For she was a true daughter of that fine woman, Isabella, whom I can see now as I write this, facing the rebels on her horse in Segovia.

Catherine was the true Queen of England, and Queen of England she would remain; particularly under the shocking circumstance, of which she was well aware, that her husband's weakness had enslaved him to the monstrous demand of the young Howard woman.

It was impossible for the Pope, under the circumstances, to solve this heavy political difficulty one way or the other at this stage, with Catherine resisting; it was impossible for the Canon lawyers, whether their interpretation of the facts and of the Pope's dispensation lay one way or the other, to terminate the proceedings at that stage. Catherine's firm will prolonged delay in the proceedings, by appeal and all the rest of it. Her abject Henry, thus subject to Anne's continued refusal to be his mere mistress as her sister had been, was goaded to final measures by the delay. Wolsey was disgraced, fell, and died. A dependent of his, the able but unscrupulous son of a Putney public-house keeper, called Cromwell, seized the moment to put himself forward.

This Cromwell (Thomas was his Christian name) had been an adventurer in Italy, had become a money-lender, had some little acquaintance with Europe and with foreign examples. He suggested to Henry the first move, not for breaking with the Papacy—nobody as yet had any idea of *that*—but for bringing special pressure to bear upon the Pope. He suggested that Henry should take the opinion of the European Universities, and, by heavy bribery, obtain at least some verdicts in his favour from them. He did, as a fact, gather a large number of University decisions in his support. To this act succeeded a number of others, *not* aimed at breaking with the Pope, but *threatening* him with a breach, and so attempting to force from him a favourable decision—

that is, a verdict against Catherine, and for Henry's plea.

Step by step, each following at intervals of a few months, the process went on. Parts of the Papal revenue were held back. Bulls from Rome were refused admission. The pressure grew heavier and heavier, but the Pope could not and would not yield. It would have been a denial of his office to have yielded while the case was still under Catherine's appeal. On the death of the Archbishop of Canterbury Henry nominated to the Primacy of the Church of England the subservient Chaplain and friend of Anne Boleyn's family, a certain Cranmer. He was a man attracted by the new German Movement, but, as the event showed, quite indifferent to what he did or said so long as he could advance in his profession. He had also one sincere interest, an exercise in which he was supreme, the construction of English prose. We owe to his pen as fine English as has ever been written. Cranmer was made Archbishop in full communion with Rome, taking the solemn oath of loyalty and obedience to the Pope. He excused his later perjury by pleading a private and secret resolve to perjure himself.

There followed the last act of the drama and the true point of Revolution. Appeals to Rome were declared, not temporarily suspended, but henceforward wholly illegal in England. A statute passing to that effect, by registration in Parliament (we must understand, of course, that Parliament did not in those days make laws; it was the *King* who made laws. Parliament, in those days, was only there to assent as a matter of course. Just as to-day it is Parliament that makes laws, and the King is only there to assent). Catherine's appeal was therefore declared legally void in England (the statute itself was legally void under the Canon Law of Europe). Cranmer was appointed to try her case: she refused to admit his jurisdiction, and her marriage with the King was declared null on Cranmer's authority as Archbishop —or, to be more accurate, as delegate of the King. This was in the summer of 1533, but already since the December of 1532 Anne Boleyn had been with child. She had yielded to the King when once she was quite certain that there would be no obstacle to her crowning. She being in this condition, Henry secretly married her on or about the 25th of January, 1533.

Henry—which really means Thomas Cromwell, his instigator—had already, two years before, put before Convocation—that is, the assembly of the English clergy—the proposal that he should assume the title of supreme head of the Church of England. The clergy, concerned (many of them at least) quite as much for the sanctity of their Order as for the supremacy of the Pope, passed the resolution, with the saving clause, "so far as the law of Christ allows it." They were familiar with the King acting as supreme head in more than nine things out of ten which concerned their activities. They thought that the saving clause would still prevent the absurdity (as it was to the people of those days) of laymen accepting the supreme clerical position. But what they had done was irrevocable, though they had hardly intended it. A new lay law was made in which, without any such saving clause, Henry was defined point blank as head of the Church of England in matters spiritual as well as temporal, and the final resort of appeal in all Church matters. Parliament of course registered this crashing innovation (upon the 3rd of November, 1534) and it became law in England. The Oath of Supremacy was administered to the Bishops and the heads of the monastic establishments. It was almost universally accepted.

That this formal break with Rome was meant to be final I do not for one moment believe; nor that the people of the day regarded it as final in the sense that it would produce a separate Church in Europe, no longer part of the visible and united Church Catholic. Yet there were found some few—very few—who instinctively felt the coming consequences of what had been done, and who cared not whether it was intended to be, or was likely to be, ephemeral or not. They were determined to the death upon the principle. They were put to death as traitors. They included Fisher, Henry's old tutor; and Thomas More, the former Chancellor. Both were men of the very highest European reputation, great humanist scholars (especially the last), and their executions raised a loud and angry protest throughout Christendom.

Yet was the breach not irrevocable. It could have

been mended. Unity could have been restored, had it not been for a second act which was of permanent effect: the seizure of the Abbey Lands. For the break between the government of England and the Holy See was followed in a couple of years, and on for four years more, by the dissolution of the monasteries and convents, and the seizure of their wealth, immediately by the Treasury; ultimately (and soon) by the landed gentry, by speculators and by a number of adventurers, obscure in origin.

The unwitting character of the English separation from the Church is nowhere better seen than in the loot of ecclesiastical endowments which thus followed the quarrel between Henry and the Pope.

When I say "unwitting" I do not mean "aimless." The aim was obvious: enrichment of the looters. I mean accomplished without calculating the consequences that would follow. Thomas Cromwell, the author of this policy as he had been of the schism, had personal fortune for his motive in both cases, and, in both cases, the acquirement of that fortune by pampering the King. That it would have, ultimately, the effect of a religious revolution was not conceivable to him and his contemporaries.

The breach with Rome had been a chance act which, I repeat, would almost certainly have failed —if left undeveloped—to be permanent: it was but an episode in a violent but essentially personal and restricted struggle. It hinged wholly upon those two points: Catherine's tenacious resistance and Anne

Boleyn's equally tenacious ambition—with Henry for puppet. It had no general basis of policy behind it, still less any national feeling. But quite a short time after it had taken place Anne Boleyn herself had been put to death and Catherine of Aragon had died: all obstacles to reconciliation has disappeared. Henry—and England—abhorred essential doctrinal change; what had been done had no outward effect on national life.

The Mass went on as usual, the Sacraments, the daily life of a somewhat slack but thoroughly Catholic populace was, on its religious side, exactly what it had been for generations. Every one had heard or read of past quarrels between King and Pope, or Papal claims. This was but another. It would blow over. Other sovereigns had threatened to break with the Pope—the King of France in particular. It had all come right in the end.

But the dissolution first of the lesser, then of *all* the Monasteries, and the later seizure of much other clerical endowment, made the breach with Rome continue. A strong motive for prolonging it was henceforward present in the wealthier and governing classes. Not that renewed communion with Rome could necessarily mean restoration of the stolen land. In point of fact, when communion was, for a few years, restored the looted property was left in the hands of its new owners. But that the old full religious life would *tend* to create, sooner or later a demand for the reparation of sacrilege, to ruin the new millionaires and to diminish the recently increased incomes of the older gentry who had shared in the adventure.

This second step, the loot of ecclesiastical endowment, was not designed as a profound religious change. There was no deep-seated scheme for making the breach with Rome more permanent. It was not one further step in a long process of gradual edging away from the mass of civilised Europe. It was adventitious, mechanical, a thing which was an end in itself—and that a sordid but wholly terrestrial end: the enrichment of Thomas Cromwell and (temporarily) of the Treasury.

The seizure of clerical wealth was a deed the ultimate consequences of which no one intended or foresaw.

We must begin by appreciating the fact that all over Europe not only monastic revenue, but the whole economic framework of ecclesiastical endowment was out of gear. The motive of its existence (which had been in its origins and for centuries the motive of supporting the Church in all her forms of activity) had suffered "crystallisation" like the rest of ecclesiastical things after the Black Death and especially during the fifteenth century. The revenue of a Bishopric, of a Parish Church, of a Monastery, even of a hospital or college, had come in an increasing number of cases to be a dead piece of wealth which the laity as well as the clergy of the day regarded not quite as we do stocks and shares, but almost as un-spiritually. Thus it was the commonest thing in the world for a great family, or the king, to apportion the revenues of some important monastery to a younger son or other relative, leaving a small amount for the local clergy who actually did the work: and you had boys (such as the young nephew of Guise, in France) made nominal abbots of houses as important as Cluny, the revenues paid to them as their private income, and no more than a stipend left over for the monk who took over the work of the office. This was true not only of monastic establishments but also of bishoprics and collegiate foundations. A man who desired to get together a large income frequently held several units of ecclesiastical endowment, leaving the episcopal work to a *locum tenens*. The whole thing had become warped in its character and divorced from its original purpose.

Oddly enough England, the only great country [1] in which there was to be a *complete* stamping out of monasticism and the one in which the most thorough loot of all other forms of clerical wealth was to take place, was also the country in which there was—at the time of the great peril—least corruption of this kind. Scotland was rotten with it, and that is why

---

[1] In the Germanies it was partial: only in the north, though not every-where, even there. In the Netherlands it only took place in seven prov-inces. In France after heavy fighting, such monastic land as had been seized was in the main restored. But in England no man could know from 1540 to the nineteenth century what the monastic life might be. It was wiped out at one blow.

the Reformation in Scotland had, when it tardily arrived, a real popular backing.

In Scotland the popular backing of disunion was at the beginning only the backing of a minority—yet it was that of an enthusiastic minority. In England the abuse of giving the revenues of the great monasteries to laymen and of putting chance adventurers into the great Sees was far less practised than anywhere else in Christendom; but all over Christendom the idea of interfering with, changing, reducing ecclesiastical revenues was prevalent, and the most orthodox reformers within the Church were as familiar with that idea as the most iconoclastic.

It must not be imagined that the suppression of a religious House was an innovation brought in by the Reformation. Wolsey, for instance, in England, had obtained leave from Rome to suppress a number of small Houses in order to endow with their revenues his great new College at Oxford, and there had been talk of further suppression for the endowment of certain new Bishoprics which were needed. It is to be noted that in this suppression of Monasteries before the Reformation the thing was undertaken as a matter of course and without noticeable protest. Wolsey had used as his agent in such orthodox suppressions that same Thomas Cromwell, who later suggested wholesale suppression to the King and was the active author of the great robbery. The idea then of suppressing a monastic body, putting its former inmates into other Houses, using its revenue for some new purpose, was quite familiar to everybody, apart from any idea of attack upon the traditional religion of the nation.

Further, I think it true in spite of certain adverse evidence that the first dissolution, the suppression of the smaller monasteries, was hardly deliberately planned as a step intended to lead on to suppressing the whole body. It seems rather that the first step raised an appetite which led to the second. The phrases used at the time, and the rules drawn up, were all of them such as had been familiar to people long before there was any question of a breach with Rome. Thus the definition of a smaller Monastery as one that had not more than twelve inmates was set forth in the permission received from Rome by Wolsey long before any one dreamt of breaking with the Pope, and the motives for suppression, or at any rate, the alleged motives—that the smaller Monasteries could not look after their affairs properly, that they were isolated, their discipline slack, etc.—were repeated in this new move as they had been in the older ones. Further, the same machinery was used for assessing the value of the rents attached to the Monasteries, and all other valuables.

When, therefore, the law was made by Henry at the suggestion of Thomas Cromwell, and duly registered by his Parliament, that the smaller Monasteries should be suppressed, the average Catholic Englishman of the day, though perhaps in places shocked by the disappearance of something with which he was familiar, and, in the case of some of the public men, shocked by the thoroughness of the affair—the destruction of all the smaller monasteries in one sweep —yet was not struck as by a *religious* change. He felt about it, to draw a distant parallel, something like what the users of a modern railway line might feel at the suppression of a very large number of small railway stations which—it might be pleaded—were no longer of use under modern conditions.

But this first move having been taken, there followed a very much more serious one, the dissolution of the larger Monasteries, the suppression of the *whole* monastic system in England, and the beginning of interference with ecclesiastical revenue other than monastic and collegiate. What was the main motive of this, the second and really revolutionary change?

It was, as I have said, almost purely financial. There may have been mixed up with it to some extent the feeling that the monks were in many cases attached to the Papal power and would irk the government as long as the quarrel with Rome lasted. Certain Houses, notably the London Carthusians, had resisted separation from Rome, one or two of the great abbots had hesitated to take the oath of supremacy, though all but a very few had at last accepted it. But that the suppression of the greater Monasteries, and the other forms of ecclesiastical loot, were *mainly* connected with the separation from Rome is a false view. That separation had made the tremendous change possible, for it gave the King what the Pope had had before, the power to license a suppression. But though one or two contemporary phrases may be gathered to that effect, the main motive was not mainly ecclesiastical, and in no way doctrinal. Thomas Cromwell himself was called by many a heretic. The Monasteries took such a large place in religious life that their sudden absence provoked indignation and widespread rebellion. But the English people did not think of the affair as a blow struck at the system of belief in which they had all grown up and took for granted. To put it in the concrete, they would never connect the suppression of the Monasteries with so astonishing an effect as the suppression of the Mass. What they did appreciate was that a very large *economic* revolution was intended.

The revenue of the Crown was increasingly insufficient in this early sixteenth century. Why this should have been so it is very difficult to determine, and I have no place for the discussion of it here. At any rate, so it was. Henry VIII, to maintain his general policy in Europe, and the management of affairs at home, was compelled to every expedient before he died: to falsifying currency, to forced loans, to imposing taxes far heavier than any of his immediate predecessors had been able to gather. There was a sort of permanent financial crisis, for expenditure was always outrunning revenue. This was the real driving power of the great change called the dissolution of the larger Monasteries.

The dissolution of the smaller Monasteries had not

affected monasticism as a whole: it remained intact. The dispossessed monks could be drafted into the larger Houses, and it was the larger Houses that represented the institution in the public eye. But when it came to the suppression of the larger Houses as a whole, and throughout the land, it was what I have called it, a revolution. A religious revolution because communal religious life suddenly ceased: an economic revolution because the Crown became suddenly possessed of a vast capital sum, one which should have sufficed for all its needs.

What proportion the whole of this ecclesiastical loot in rents, precious metals and movable wealth bore to the surplus wealth of the country, that is, to the wealth of the governing classes as a whole, it is very difficult to say. Popular tradition put it down at one-third. It probably was not that, but it may have been one-fifth. We have here one of those very difficult problems which history is perpetually presenting, in which two bodies of evidence are in conflict. If we consider only the assessment of wealth as detailed in the ecclesiastical valuations, we get a sum obviously far less than that which the Crown really seized. For though the estimate of one-third, or even one-fifth, may be too much, there cannot have been such a universal sense of the magnitude of the revolution and such a tradition of the vastness of the confiscation unless it had really been very great.

Personally, I believe it was probably about a fifth; not, of course, of the whole wealth of the country but, as I have said, of the *surplus* wealth, that is, of the wealth which supported the manorial lords and the corporate bodies and so forth over and above what supported the labouring mass of the nation.

Further, we can see for ourselves in the indirect later effects of the change (such as the new palaces of those who ultimately received the Church lands) on what a scale the confiscation was. Whatever it was, however, whether one-fifth or a sixth, or only a seventh, it had two effects. First, it made reconciliation with Rome in any permanent fashion far more difficult. Secondly, it upset the economic balance of the country, first making the Crown for a very short time far more powerful, and then, when the new wealth had been dissipated among new adventurers and old landed families, gradually throwing the balance of economic power into the hands of a greatly enriched upper class, which, in a century, destroyed the monarchy.

If Henry had kept the wealth which thus accrued to him, if it had become a permanent endowment of the Crown, the English popular monarchy would have become the most powerful in Europe.

But he did not keep it. He did not keep it for several reasons. First of all for this reason, the most important, his own character; the character of a weak, violent, spendthrift man, capable of throwing money about as had none of his predecessors, perpetually gambling, giving away estates to his favourites, the sport of impulse. Next because the Crown was

in such embarrassment that it was strongly tempted
to realise its new wealth, and quickly sold monastic
land and other goods at prices far too low. Often
the nominal price at which it sold (it actually realised less) was only ten years' purchase, whereas the
normal rate was twenty years' purchase. Next there
was the fact that even a very powerful popular monarchy, such as Henry's, could not carry through a
revolution so sudden and so gigantic, without relying
upon the directing men of his time, the adventurers
whom he had gathered about him, the old nobility,
the squires and great merchants in the House of Com-
mons, and sundry astute industrious clerks and hangers-on who had a keen eye for their own advantage.

Thus Thomas Cromwell himself kept a vast amount
of monastic wealth for his private use. He not only
did that, but he gave his nephew quantities of it, con-
structing for him an enormous fortune, which was
the basis of the Cromwell family, and the origin of
Oliver's importance a hundred years later. Of the
county members in the Reformation Parliament there
was not *one* who did not share in the loot. These and
other causes led to the very rapid dispersion of the
ecclesiastical wealth which Henry had seized.

No thorough analysis has ever been made, nor perhaps is one possible; for the records, though very numerous, are far from covering the whole ground.
But industrious workers have made it fairly certain
that more than half the wealth had gone from the
Crown before Henry died. Immediately after his

death, under Edward VI, as I shall point out later, masses more were seized. Mary gave hardly anything away, but Elizabeth, being in the hands of this now newly enriched class, had to surrender land to them right and left; to be more accurate, they took it from her.

Before two lifetimes had elapsed, very nearly the whole of the loot had left the hands of the impoverished Crown, and was in the power of the new millionaires, and their landed class had already begun to govern England and to destroy the old popular monarchy of the English.

CHAPTER III

Calvin

I N that same year, when Henry of England, at Thomas Cromwell's suggestion, began the dissolution of the monasteries, there appeared a book which was destined to make all the difference to the fortunes of the Reformation, and to give consistency and form, and therefore endurance, to the fatal cleavage of Christendom.

This book was the "Institute" [1] written by a Frenchman of Noyon: one Jean Cauvin.

Men sometimes talk of a book as having changed the world. The talk is usually exaggerated, and even off the mark. More often a book of great effect is but the exposition, the putting into clear form, of ideas already widely received. Often, again, a book gets great historical standing as a cause, when it is no more than the registration of some institution already founded, and bound to continue with equal vigour whether the book had been compiled or no.

But in the case of this book of John Calvin's (to use the English form of the name) we come as near as we can anywhere in history to a piece of writing which was itself an agent, and a single agent.

Even here we must not exaggerate. The effect of

[1] "Christianæ Religionis Institutio."

the book was principally due to its coming when it did: it exactly supplied what was needed; it cast the Reformation into a mould at a moment when the movement was still fluid, while the crucible was still boiling. The same book produced to-day would have no such effect. The same book produced in the thirteenth century would have had a great effect, but not the same effect.

Nevertheless it is true that the Institute of John Calvin did far more to stamp, mould and render permanent the thing which we have known for more than three hundred years as "Protestantism" (the ethical mood which has been of such powerful effect upon the history of our race) than any other factors of the Reformation; and that truth is an excellent proof that the mind of man lives by doctrine, and that clear thought is the master of mere emotion. Until that book appeared the Reformation had, for now twenty years, lived upon Protest against, and indignation with, the later abuses of the Church. Its doctrines had been various and confused, its course devious: an eddy.

What Calvin did was to produce a church, a creed, a discipline, which could be set over against what had been for all these centuries (and what still is) the native church, creed, and discipline of Christian civilisation. For John Calvin it was who produced, down to its details with the rapidity of genius, and with the tenacity of genius, a new thing.

True, great bodies of Europeans broke away permanently from unity, yet would not wholly follow Calvin. Such was the Lutheran mass; such, of course, were the bulk of English Protestants to be; and even among those who were profoundly influenced by the "fundamental brain-work" of this man, whole groups —such as the Independents of the seventeenth century—refused to conform to the rigid framework he had established.

Yet it remains true that Calvinism is the core of Protestantism to this day; that the effects on character which the Protestant culture continues to admire are essentially the effects of Calvinism; that the whole world of anti-Catholic thought, even to-day when it has lost the doctrines of Calvinism, is in its most intimate ideals moulded on the Calvinistic model.

What Calvin did was this. He took what is one of the oldest and most perilous directives of mankind, *the sense of Fate.* He isolated it, and he made it supreme, by fitting it with the kneading of a powerful mind, into the scheme which Christian men still traditionally associated with the holiness and authority of their ancestral religion.

God had become Man, and God had become Man to redeem mankind. That was no part of the old idea of Inevitable Fate. On the contrary, it was a relief from that pagan nightmare. We of the Faith say that the Incarnation was intended to release us from such a pagan nightmare. Well, Calvin accepted the

Incarnation, but he forced it to fit in with the old pagan horror of compulsion: "Ananke." He reintroduced the Inexorable.

Yes, God had become Man and had died to save mankind; but only mankind in such numbers and persons as he had chosen to act for. The idea of the Inexorable remained. The merits of Christ were imputed, and no more. God was Causation, and Causation is one immutable whole. A man was damned or saved; and it was not of his doing. The recognition of evil as equal with good, which rapidly becomes the worship of evil (the great Manichean heresy, which has roots as old as mankind; the permanent motive of Fear) was put forward by Calvin in a strange new form. He did not indeed oppose, as had the Manichean, two equal principles of Good and of Evil. He put forward only one principle, God. But to that One Principle he ascribed all our suffering, and, for most of us, necessary and eternal suffering.

Again the Catholic Church had called the soul of man immortal. Calvin accepted that doctrine; but under his hands it becomes an immortality of doom, and for the few who shall have doom to beatitude, doom it yet is, as doom it is to the myriads for whom it shall mean despair.

From this great man, I say, proceeds a whole web of ideas which still live, though the doctrines which were so living to him and his followers, the strict dogmas upon which they evolved their mighty system of warped theology, have faded from the modern mind.

Calvin

If to-day your non-Catholic conceives of the material, and, more latterly, the spiritual processes as inevitable, if he inclines to despair, if he is tempted by
the latest fad of the "sub-conscious" which man fights
in vain, the savour of Calvin is in it all.

You may find to-day in unexpected regions of
thought the influence of the man. He it was, for
instance, who said that the ministry must proceed
from election, but that ministers once elected had
authority over the electors. What better parallel for
the Parliamentary fallacy, the falsity of which Europe
is only now perceiving? He it was who in a fashion
not general, like that of the old humanist scholars, but
direct and dogmatic, pitted document, however frag-
mentary, against the living voice of tradition. He it
was who rendered humility futile and the appetite
for wealth a virtue. He it was who began the war
against *Joy*. He it was who set up in so definite a
fashion the wall which separates the Catholic mind
in Europe from its opponents; he it was who put up
a new positive force directed against the positive force
of the Catholic Church.

It is an extraordinary story. The book was produced by a very young man—he was only twenty-
five when it appeared. It was produced by a young
man, who after some seven or eight years of academic
seclusion had covered with incredible industry and
with the minute accuracy in a retentive memory the
whole field of studies necessary for his object.

He was not the only Picard [2] in history to show lucidity, coldness, and rigidity of plan. His fellow countryman Robespierre is another famous example (for his Artois is indistinguishable from Picardy). It was the French spirit, but the northern French, the less generous, the people that have no vineyards, which produced Jean Cauvin.[3]

If we ask what it was in Calvin's doctrine, apart from the opportuneness of its moment and its effect against the clergy which gave it so much power, the answer is, I think, that it provided an awful object of worship and that it appealed at the same time to a powerful human appetite which Catholicism opposes. The novel object was an implacable God, the appetite was love of money. There is a dark instinct of horror which is found lurking or patent, in all antiquity and modern pagan ritual, a demand for victims and a prostration before dreadful power. Calvin provided victims. For his ardent disciples, remember, were elect. It was the others who were damned, and as for love of money, a philosophy which decided good works and dreaded abnegation let it loose in all its violence. Calvinism had men enrich themselves and they have done so.

[2] His birthplace, Noyon, is only on the confines of Picardy, not in it. But its character is of those desolate plains.

[3] As was the contemporary habit among scholars the name *Cauvin* (which means "Baldhead") was Latinised into *"Calvinus."* The Germans so called him. The French re-turned it into "Calvin" which form the English copied. It must be noted that contemporaries sometimes write the family name as "Calvin."

He lived on with increasing, untiring, widely and more widely spreading effect. He made of Geneva another Rome. He provided a pole of energy and a nucleus for the struggle that was opening against orthodoxy; but he did it by making a new orthodoxy which was an armour.

Few read the Institute to-day; yet any one who wishes to understand the great rift which opened in Europe should acquaint himself with at least the most significant part of that work. There is an excellent English translation by Allen, published in the midst of the nineteenth century; and he who will turn to it may find all those characters I have described.

He will also find, if he will keep a perfectly detached mind, what all Calvin's followers, and even most of his critics, deny; and that is, the curious occasional failures in sincerity which are so native to the system-maker. He evidently first had his system produced in his mind, and then compelled evidence to fit in. This is most notably the case in his appeals to St. Augustine; and especially in his wobbling over the word Sacrifice in connection with the Eucharist. Read carefully the eighteenth chapter of the Fourth Book, and see if this is not so. You have the same shirking or gliding over or minimising of evidence in the third chapter of the same, where he tries to make out a case for the election of the ministry. As for that strange delight in vengeance, or what we may call Divine Justice, but which he certainly thinks of as Divine *Necessity,* be pleased to consider the little passage on the torments of Hell in the twenty-fifth chapter of the Second.

Calvin, then, came forth in this year 1536 with the book, accompanied by a letter to his Prince (Francis I, King of France) which did the work: hardened, erected, embattled the attack upon the Ancient Mother.

But if we ask why that book produced so enormous an effect in its first few years, and why by the middle of the century it had turned France into a battle-ground, began to sweep Scotland, and a lifetime later to shake England, the answer is here, once more, as throughout the Reformation, *the attack on priest-hood.*

The vague, impetuous, chaotic, original German movement, the older quarrel with communion under one kind, the yet older denial of sacramental power to sinful priests, the tendency to substitute the dead Scriptural authority for the old living authority— all these things were rooted in one common driving force, which was reaction against the conception of a sacrificing priesthood, and of an order sacramentally set apart for the exercise of spiritual power among Christian men. Hitherto no *system* had co-ordinated and made clear these confused protests which arise, as we have seen, out of indignation with the corruption of the clergy. The acute rebellion of life against mechanism, driven by that undying hatred of the Faith itself, which the very power of Faith produces, had produced a negative result of disunion and confusion. So much had been the German work. Here, after twenty years of it, came forth this strong and disciplined French mind, Calvin, presenting entire a system which explained in a full and worked-out philosophy how one might be rid of the Priest, and against the hated creed and discipline set up another discipline and creed. Upon that was the public fortune of his book founded.

A book even with the active work of a man behind the book, takes some years to produce its effect. Calvin's blow had been delivered in 1536. After four years the fissure that blow had started began to broaden perceptibly.

Up to 1540 the Reformation movement, which to-day appears to us as the division of Europe into two sharply divided societies, had remained a *general* discussion. The *Social* Union of Europe was still taken for granted.

The ten years that follow were the gradual permeation of Europe with the effects of a new philosophy. Hitherto men growing up from youth to middle age had been plunged into a wrangle. Now they were tending to separate into two camps. It was the winding up of this "Period of Debate."

Yet during the decade between 1540 and 1549, the overwhelming issue, whether Christendom should remain united or no, still remained doubtful. The time was still a time of argument, dependent upon persuasion and example, rhetoric, and as yet, only the *disconnected* use of force. At the same time, it remained a phase of cross-currents. In England orthodox doctrine was preserved, while political separation from Rome was emphasised; in France doctrine, the main issue, was confused by the needs of the monarchy and its rivalry with the Emperor (Charles V), the Catholic champion; in the many principalities and cities of the Germans was a growing tendency to admit the impossibility of any solution—the fatal policy of despair and final acceptation of division was gathering strength. But throughout them all nothing was yet fixed. There were not, *as yet,* two opposed forces in Christendom. Everything remained in flux, though in a flux which was showing signs of settling into two bodies.

We are mainly concerned with three units, France, England, and the Empire—counting, of course, the Swiss Cantons as a fringe of the Imperial system. The Spaniards had been little affected by the revolt, because their whole soul was concentrated upon preserving the arduous reconquest of their Christian land against the Mohammedan and his Jewish allies; hence the intensity of their Inquisition. In Italy the high flood of the Renaissance made men sceptical and contemptuous of what they thought such puerilities as the unique appeal to Scripture and the spinning of new theological systems. In Scotland the fire had not yet been lit. The main strategic field, the Low Countries, had not yet come into play.

But among the Germans, the French and the English, the debate of the Reformation was in its last stages from 1540 to 1549, and to understand its future fortunes we must know how it fared during those ten years, in each district, with the generation which had seen the beginning of the movement in youth and was now approaching age. For a man of, say, 21, when Luther's first protest was heard, a man whose formative years between 12 and 20 had been filled with the quarrel of Humanist and Scholastic, novel culture and old tradition, was, by 1549, grown to be over 50; he was joining the generation of the old, and yet newer things were pressing on him. Such men had no experience of disunion and could not conceive it. But Calvin's leaven was at work upon their sons, and their sons were to achieve the splitting of Europe.

The first district to judge is the French; for France is about to become the battlefield, whereupon it is to be decided whether the Catholic Church shall, humanly speaking, survive or no; and it was in France that Calvin's work is beginning to pierce with most acuity.

The next to be remarked is England. Here a strange political accident had had the double effect of affirming the sanctity of the old and united Catholic doctrine as it had nowhere else been affirmed—consistently, universally, and with the crushing of all opposition [4]—and an equally clear and violent separation from the centre of doctrinal unity—the Pa-

---

[4] Henry VIII actually made it a penal offence to shirk confession!

pacy. Here, in England, was Calvin's effect least felt. Yet here also had come, as nowhere else, the destruction of the monastic institution, which was the main social support of Catholic unity; and this destruction had been accompanied by the loot of those endowments which were the chief temporal strength of religion.

Lastly, we have the Germans. Among them also Calvin, though more effective than in England, had not yet worked on as he already had on France. The Germanies were still under the impulse of their original confused movement, with over twenty years of momentum behind it. They had experience of Princes and Cities successfully defying the Crown, and this last phase of the debate in Germany was a surrender to the rebels. We have seen how there was here no strong central power, as there was in France and England. The Turkish peril, as we have also seen, had paralysed the last poor opportunities of the Emperor, the nominal King of all Germans, to impose his will.

Let us consider these three fields, France, England, Germany, in more detail during this last phase in "The Period of Debate"—the years just preceding 1547-1549; the years during which Calvin's book continued to increase in influence.

As to the French, it is especially to be observed that with them there had begun long before Luther an attempt at reform *within* the Church. I do not say that it was not perilous; but I will affirm that it was orthodox. Men like Lefèvre of Etaples, and the Bishop of Meaux, and their followers, had set the current towards a rational reform, a settlement of the monstrous abuses, a putting of Christian society upon its feet again, a fostering of personal religious feeling, which need in no way have destroyed unity, but rather (no doubt after much and violent discussion) have early produced what was later produced— *a Reform of the Church from within*—the Church purified of iniquities in personnel, of anomalies in practice and of abuses in custom, but with her full personal and holy individuality not only preserved but revived.

But that original effort at internal reform, of which the French were (characteristically) the founders, failed. The Lutheran propaganda from Germany had early seized upon a few wild men in France; placards insulting the central institution of Christian men, the Mass, had violently offended the people of Paris and had provoked very strong reprisals. Then had come Calvin's book; and after that for fifteen years Calvin's book began to produce a stronger and still stronger definite organisation to oppose the Faith.

The first organised Calvinist Church of real importance, that of Rouen, dates from 1546, ten years after the book, and thenceforward they spring up everywhere, beginning to make a little State within the State. By 1547 Francis I, whose own relatives had had leanings towards the new enthusiasm, but who himself was convincedly and sincerely Catholic, whose pre-occupation was not with the new religious quarrel, but with Charles V and the arms of the German Empire, whose whole attitude and policy had been confused between discordant objects, and had so allowed the Calvinist movement to obtain a foothold, was dead.

In England, Henry had maintained (with the full force of the State, the support of most of his subservient prelates, and most certainly that of the populace, which loathed heresy) the main body of Catholic orthodoxy.[5]

Our official textbooks for school and university use are written as though England were then—1540-1547—wavering between the full tradition of the Catholic Church and a plunge into the German anarchy, or later into the Calvinist "Counter-Church." That is not history. It is anti-Catholic propaganda, imposed by the modern system of compulsory examination, and designed to present Protestantism as something native to the English mind. The historical truth is that though there could not but be plenty of discussion on what was agitating all Europe, just as there is plenty of discussion on Communism to-day, the mass of the English people were, as yet, less affected by the anarchic anti-Catholic movement than any in Europe and by the new organised anti-Catholicism of Calvin hardly at all. Only a group of

[5] On one point, Henry, out of a political feeling, wobbled the full doctrine of Purgatory and Masses for the dead. But there is no doubt of his private feelings.

intellectuals with their few followers had been touched as yet by *that* enthusiasm.

Apart from a handful of wild men and women such as you get in any moment of excited discussion, those who in very different degrees attacked any part of Catholic doctrine were an unpopular minority, divided between an academic clique—powerful through the intelligence and clerical position of its members—and the group—very large and increasing —of those who had been allowed to share with Henry the loot of the Church lands.

These, indeed, felt more and more the necessity of preventing reunion with the Church. They owed their position to the dissolution of the monasteries, just as the opportunity of the academic reformers (such as Ridley) had been given them by the breach with Rome. But the whole mass of the English people was behind the King during all these last years of his—1540-1547—in his determination to retain in vigour the main body of Catholic practice and doctrine. Henry's marriage with Anne of Cleves failed, and was never a real approach to the German movement of disunion; and it is possible, or probable, that when he died—much at the same time as Francis—he was again considering reconciliation with the Papal See.

Of the Germans the story can be more simply told. The Emperor had never had the power to maintain unity, for the Germans were a united people, as indeed they have never been before or since; having, as it would seem, a distaste for organised nationality, though a strong feeling of race. The "protesting" bodies, that is, the rulers and cities which attacked the old united society of Christendom and set out upon a new and varied religious speculation (with spoliation of Church goods accompanying and confirming them), formed at first a league which was defeated; but the defeat was in no way decisive. The anxiety of the Emperor and his brother of Austria was for compromise, for religious truce, not for the victory of Faith. "*Interims*" appeared (the word *Interim* is Latin for "meanwhile") —first that of Ratisbon, then that of Augsburg, and these "*Interims*" were armistice negotiations, the whole spirit of which was the fatal admission that the Catholic Church and its now numerous and allied opponents might treat one with the other as equal parties in an admitted break-up of Europe. In other words, with the Germans, Catholic social unity had, for the moment, disappeared, while it still stood firm in France and England.

The *Interim* of Augsburg comes shortly after the death of Francis I of France and of Henry VIII of England, and with it this period in Germany ends. As we approach the middle date of the sixteenth century, therefore, we approach the end of the first clear, large phase in the story of the Reformation, which I have called "The Period of Debate."

What was to follow it was the "Period of Conflict." But in between came ten years or somewhat more

(1547-49 to 1559), during which the forces were lining up for active battle, which I will call "The Preliminaries of Conflict."

At this point in the story of the Reformation, 1547-1549, let us pause and sum up the situation. For it is the close of the first main division in the process of disunion.

Calvin's book has been out a dozen years. Those who were filled with it in youth are now active men in the thirties, stirring Europe.

Henry of England, Francis of France, the strong defenders of the Mass have been dead two years. The miserable German compromise of Augsburg has just been made, and the governmental attack on the Mass has begun in England.

How did men feel at this moment? How far had progressed the increasing peril of Christendom by 1549?

There had hitherto been, taking Europe as a whole, a wide freedom of expression. There had been quarrelling of the most violent sort and a *mêlée* of new national feelings, new doctrines, class hatreds, personal objects, dynastic ambitions, etc., etc. This confusion was based upon freedom of discussion, and upon the fact that there was as yet—save at the end of it in the fatal example of the Germans—no clean division of adherent and dissident, orthodox and deniers. The spirit of the time had been œcumenical; the *whole* church was to be changed, to its advantage;

or to be retained to its advantage, in the ancient form; or to admit an admixture of reform and conservation. There had been plenty of sporadic fighting, and plenty of persecuting force used; but things had not yet settled into opposing camps, still less into battle. But now—round about 1549—the full cleavage began to appear.

For ten years after, the varying parties (now more and more separated into two opposing groups) were lining up for battle. Then comes the next critical date, 1559, the sharp sudden rising in Scotland, the calling in of Elizabeth by the new millionaires in England to be their opportune head, and the grumblings of what was later to be civil war in France: very shortly after that came the business of the Low Countries upon which also the fate of unity was to turn. Up to 1549 matters had still remained open to settlement—though more and more doubtfully with each year as that date was approached. The decade between that point—1539-40—and 1549 is the beginning, but only the beginning, of the cooling and hardening in this boiling mass of protest and counter-protest, eager reformer, followers eager or sluggish in their various degrees, men instinctively and sharply rallied to defend the Faith (such men as Beda, to-day not sufficiently praised for his foresight and loyalty) and the rest of it.

Well, then, how did the average man in Europe think of the European affair at this turning-point, the middle of the sixteenth century?

He knew nothing, of course, of the complete separation that was ultimately to come. But the idea
of "Protestant" as opposed to "Catholic" was already
beginning to be familiar to him, but not in the form
of opposing cultures, still less of opposing geographical divisions in Europe. Of "Latin," "Teutonic,"
and all the rest of our false modern jargon, he was
innocent. The reality for him (and it is still the
underlying reality for all of us) was Christendom.
The varying nationalities had begun to appear, but
in very varying degrees of distinction and regarded
rather as the rights of Princes than of Peoples. Scotland was quite foreign to England, and hostile.
France was but recently united, Spain the same; Italy
was but a mass of Principates and Cities; the Germans
a still more inchoate mass of various local governments, most of them very small, under a nominal
supremacy of the Emperor. The Mohammedan had
already attempted to force the gates of Europe, and
might at any moment break in.

As for doctrine (the one essential point) the men
of 1549 were still in the full fervour of individual
dialectic, argument, theory and affirmation. Lutheran and Zwinglian were still at odds upon the
Sacrament, and Anabaptists against both, with dozens
of other tendencies: all of course, agreeing to attack
the traditional organisation of Christians under the
Papacy, and the majestic structure of the universal
Church. Into all this had been thrust the hard wedge
of Calvin's book with its immense effects of doctrine,

organisation, and counter-church, set up solidly at Geneva and spreading rapidly through France. An *Institution*, the Presbyterian thing, was born.

We are accustomed in these modern days to ask upon almost any historical debate the somewhat futile question:

"Where lay the majority?" I have called it "futile" because questions are hardly ever clean-cut, and because clean-cut varies infinitely in degree, from the mass (which is generally apathetic) to the brave fanatics of the extreme wings who commonly decide the issue.

But if for the purpose of answering the question we make an analysis of the state of affairs of Europe in uproar on that date 1549, we arrive at something like this:

As to whether the old, traditional, known religion should be maintained, an overwhelming majority of Europe was still—by 1549—in favour; anything you like—ten to one, or twenty to one. In England especially was this feeling strong—stronger perhaps than it was anywhere else, outside Spain, of the single organised nations.

As to whether the Papacy were a necessary centre of unity, whether civilian rulers and the churches of their various realms and districts might not be organised without submission to it, there was a divided attitude, with chances *against* (for the moment) a majority's supporting the full Papal claim.

This attitude was strongly affected by most men's

accepting of the natural right of their civilian rulers (Kings and Princes) to command them, by the current talk and protest against recent corruptions of the Papal court and most of all by the memories of clerical taxation. On this there had been protest everywhere, grumbling everywhere, and in some places, notably in England, the feeling against paying rents and dues to the Church had been so strong, that the government could depend upon it as a weapon for terrifying the clergy.

As to the necessity for reform of abuses, the almost universal agreement among all those who were alive to such questions at all had gradually in the course of thirty years become modified by a dread lest reform might not mean (if it were undertaken too angrily) the break-up of Europe.

Meanwhile the essential thing—reform from within, which, undertaken in time would have saved Europe—still hung fire. It had begun, it was gathering strength—but it was not yet sufficient to save unity.

There we may see how the thing would have looked, judged as we judge to-day by vague majorities—a bad way of judging, *even* when we analyse those majorities.

But when it comes to noting the centres of intensity, the poles of energy, the foci, the points of leadership, in 1549 *there* the issue was already definite, although real battle was not yet joined.

The issue was between two forces. On the one

hand was the instinct which we all have within us, that Europe is Catholic, must live as Catholic, or must die; that in the anarchic religious rebellion was peril of death to our art, our culture, to that from which they proceed, our religious vision. On the other had arisen an intense, fierce, increasing hatred against the Mass, the Blessed Sacrament, the whole transcendental scheme; a hatred such that all who felt it were, in spite of a myriad differences, in common alliance. That hatred fed upon an original popular indignation against the corruption of the clergy, and especially against their financial claims. But the hatred was far older than any such late medieval trouble; it was as old as the presence of the Catholic Church in this world. It was as old as the beginnings of Predication of Jesus Christ in Galilee. It had been given an organisation, a Philosophy, Staffwork and a core by the genius of Calvin.

The Catholic conscience, the oppressing hatred of the Catholic faith, were now—at this central point in the sixteenth century—about to join issue, to provoke battle, and to end by surrendering our culture into two opposing worlds which stand enemies to this day.

CHAPTER IV

The Lining Up for Battle: 1549-1559

IT is the mid-sixteenth century. Time had had its effect on so prolonged a quarrel. It had now occupied over thirty years. It had covered the active part of men's lifetimes. The younger generation had grown up in an air of spiritual combat. That combat was about to become physical.

Henry VIII of England and Francis I of France, who had defended the Mass, were dead. The Emperor Charles V was about to resign and divide his dominions. All was expectant of a clash: a trial of strength.

Therefore the following ten years, from 1549 to 1559, bear a new complexion; the forces are beginning to line up for battle.

The critical fields of the Reformation are France, England, Germany, and the Netherlands.

Each of these four plays a special part. Germany was the originator, and in Germany, from lack of a central government, the revolt against European unity was able to establish itself. The Netherlands were the strategical point. They were the military key to the position. Had authority achieved a complete instead of only a partial victory in the Netherlands, the final disruption of Christendom would not have taken place. But Germany and the Netherlands take a later part in the conflict. The "lining up for battle" was mainly the affair of France and England, and with these we will here deal.

The first thing we have to seize in the tumultuous sequence of political and religious happenings between 1549 and 1559 in England, is that we are watching successive Central Governments, each of a despotic power such as was not exercised in any other large European state. This it is essential to grasp, or no meaning could be made of that strange time. By so much as in the Germanies central power was lacking, by so much in England was it absolute, immediate and supreme. It so remained throughout the reign of Henry VIII, throughout the brief tyranny of "The Council" which ordered all things under the nominal boy-King, Edward VI, and throughout the reign of Mary. After Mary—who died at the end of this critical ten years—the new fortunes began to master the Crown.

The English people had become the passive subjects of such a Central Government from a number of causes, the three chief of which were: (1) The absence, after a lifetime of civil war and usurpation, of a class rich enough, large enough, and organised enough to fight Henry VIII. (2) The fact that Henry, while making possible *any* religious change by his breach with Rome, did not interfere with the daily, ordinary religion of Englishmen during the long fourteen years of his remaining life. This lulled men into an acceptance of Government orders in religion—until it was too late. (3) The monopoly of artillery and gunpowder (and printing) in the hands of Government. (4) The fact that *at first* the richer classes, which would have been the natural leaders of a revolt against tyranny, had been tamed to accept it by the opportunities it had given them of sudden enrichment through the loot of religion. Later this newly-enriched class became too strong for the monarchy, undermined it under Elizabeth and James, and destroyed it under Charles. But up to 1559 the body of fortunes suddenly swollen by Church wealth felt their wealth to be pouring from the Crown, the unquestioned power of which they therefore supported until they began to discover their own strength upon Mary's death. After which the doom of Monarchy, as yet far distant, was certain.

As to the purely religious question, England till 1549 had hardly been troubled. Though the enemies in England (principally Calvinist) of Catholic practice and mind had acquired considerable strength underground, as it were, during Henry's last years of despotism, yet they remained, till 1559 and long after, a small and unpopular minority.

Nevertheless, the exceedingly strong central government in England did, after Henry VIII's death, successfully play at a violent but brief religious revolution. The few rich men in power under the nominal rule of Young Edward, after first translating the

Mass into English, next suppressed it for three years, and just managed to put down, largely with foreign mercenaries, the consequent popular revolts.

The motive of that unnatural attack upon the general traditions of the English was, what has always thrown society upside down, a sudden accidental opportunity of making yet another batch of vast new fortunes and adding to the old.

When Henry had looted the Church wealth, enormous as the operation was, the average man thought of it as a confiscation by the Crown, an idea with which he was familiar. That wealth had already been largely lost to the Crown, and dissipated among the squires, the great merchants, and others by the time Henry died. But your "man in the street" of the day still thought of it vaguely as the affair of the Government: and possibly as a chance for alleviating taxation sooner or later. But when Henry VIII was dead, leaving a wretched sickly child, Edward, barely ten years of age, as nominal king, that child's uncles, the Seymours, and their hangers-on, had presented to them in one enormous moment such a chance for increasing their incomes as the wildest imagination of their class had never yet dreamed of.

The Seymour brothers were by origin small squires, one might almost say, according to modern standards, not much more than big farmers. They were now (especially the eldest of them, who made himself an ephemeral despot under the title of Protector) in a position to lap up all the remaining wealth of chan-

tries, hospitals, schools, and put it into their own
pockets—theirs and their friends and cronies of the
clique. They ran for this loot as thirsty dogs run for
water. It could not be successfully enjoyed without
the destruction of Church ceremonial and magnificence. With the help of Cranmer the Archbishop
they destroyed that order and magnificence. First
the Seymour Government and its successor translated
the Mass into English in a new "Prayer Book," modified it, confiscated its endowment and the wealth of
its ritual and shrines in jewellery, tapestry, furniture,
plate and building. These they took for themselves.
Then they, in 1552, imposed upon the people of England a new ceremonial of religion, in a second Prayer
Book; and at a blow abolished the last vestiges of the
Mass which they had already undermined.

There were great popular risings all over the place
—risings put down, as I have said, largely by the use
of foreign mercenaries, and with the most horrible
cruelty. So formidable were these in West England
as in East, that had the Governmental power been
less centralised they would have created, as in France
later, a lasting civil war. But they lacked gentry to
lead them—for the gentry, since the loot of the
Abbey Lands, had a vested interest in the new state
of affairs, and the bulk of them abandoned the English people in their fight for their fathers' faith.
These risings had economic grievances behind them
also; but the leaven which raised the people so to
combat an all-powerful artillery and organisation was

the sudden attempt at destroying their traditional religion.

How far the attempt at doing this would have succeeded, after years of oppression, we cannot tell, for the experiment was happily cut short by the child-King's death. The diseased little fellow is made a great pother about in our books, but he was really of no consequence. He was but a toy in the hands of the despoilers.

When he was dying, a rival clique of rich men had managed to get rid of Seymour—as he had already got rid of his own brother and rival. They had done it through the treason of one William Cecil (son of an official and grandson of a publican in Stamford) on whom we must keep an eye: for in a few years he is to govern England. He was clerk to the Governing Council, knew all its secrets and handed over Seymour to his rival Dudley. Dudley put Seymour to death to make certain of a larger income as Seymour had put his own brother to death for the same reason; and William Cecil was the directing brain in the background: the only man of the Council who worked and the man who knew all. The Dudleys, busy at new loot on their own account, tried to confirm their ill-gotten gains and power by putting forward the absurd candidature of Lady Jane Grey, on the plea that she was also descended from Henry VII, and had been brought up in the anti-Catholic clique. But Mary Tudor, the eldest daughter of Henry, and named by him to follow her brother if that brother had no issue, easily succeeded, supported as she was by a *third* great popular rising in favour of what was still rooted in men's hearts as the religion of the country. With Mary the Church was restored, and that restoration had the people behind it. A Kentish rebellion got up by the French Ambassador (for France in England, as in Germany, played for religious dissension among her rivals), and led by a man called Wyatt (son of the minor Poet who had got a mass of Church loot), failed. Mary's reign was marked by the unpopular alliance with Spain, but also by action against the anti-Catholic minority which had taken so strong a hold, through Government support, during her diseased little brother's few years.

The effort came somewhat late in her reign—that reign lasted no longer than her brother's had done—and took the form of penal legislation and executions. As for the monastic lands, it is important to note that even Mary, with the great mass of the English people behind her, could not restore them—at any rate for the moment. The organised wealth of the country—the class of squires and rich merchants—was too much involved.

Mary Tudor set out with vigour to confirm the national religion and of all that scheme of Society in which Englishmen—save for a wild interlude of five years—had lived all their lives, and their ancestors before them, since England was England. She put to work her strong repressive policy against that small but intense minority which had only been a nucleus in her father's lifetime, but had exercised a violent tyranny after it. She put to death by the age-long and legal punishment of burning nearer three than two hundred people up and down the country who refused to recant their heretical views. She took special vengeance upon Ridley and Latimer and Cranmer, and in the case of the latter that vengeance was personal, because he had been the tool of Henry VIII in the undoing of her mother, and had been the shameful servant of the policy which raised Anne Boleyn, his patroness. He was unjustly treated, for he was always ready to recant.

Had Mary lived we do not know how much longer the persecution might have continued, nor what further number of victims it might have made. I suggest that they would have been at least double in number before the repression had had its final effect, the attack on the Catholic Church, that is, on the faith of the mass of the people, stamped out, and the set which supported that attack destroyed. For that set, small as its body was in mere numbers, was in its very various and discordant tenets intensely sincere, whether they were denying the Deity altogether or the Trinity or property or the wearing of clothes, or the mystery of the Eucharist. And they had recently had such official support as had enlarged their numbers. One thing they had in common, on one all such sectaries agreed, which was their hatred of unity and of the Catholic faith.

What the sacrifice would have been before the end was reached, we cannot tell, because Mary died prematurely at the end of the year 1558.

There are two legends which it is important to discard before we leave this critical passage in the story of England: first the legend that the burning of people alive struck contemporaries with a peculiar horror, as it strikes us; secondly, the legend that the English people, largely indifferent to religion, were sickened by the active persecution of the unpopular minority and thereby turned against the faith of their fathers.

Both these legends are historically false. The proof is that even the small body which sympathised with the victims was not so much incensed against the method of punishments, as against any punishment being inflicted. But I think it is true that the scale upon which the thing was done was so exceptional as to move opinion somewhat.

Suppose to-day, in a reaction after a Communist attempt, over two thousand men who had lately been taking part in Communist activity were condemned to long years of penal servitude. There would be a feeling of novelty and surprise at so widely spread a severity and in many there would be ill-ease. To that extent I think Mary's persecution was felt to be abnormal in its degree and intensity.

But that was not the essential point at the moment. The essential point at the moment was that the very wealthy new millionaires who had battened upon the ruined Church felt that they were in danger.

Cecil, the head of them, was so frightened that he went about with a pair of rosary beads, devoutly muttering them, and from him down to the smallest man who had dealt in the stolen jewels, chalices, and patens which had held the Blessed Sacrament, no one felt safe. Therefore it was that when Mary died, in late 1558, all that very large body which had, from a few shillings to what in our day would be called millions, benefited by the loot of religion, combined not only to put Elizabeth her sister upon the throne (that was normal, because Elizabeth was the next Tudor daughter and designated so to succeed in her father, Henry's, will) but, what is much more important, to turn Elizabeth's accession into a means for gradually but tenaciously, ruthlessly uprooting the religion of the English people.

It took fifty years before half the English had become the opponents of their fathers' traditions, much more before the bulk of the nation had definitely become anti-Catholic. But after 1559 the process was continuous.

So much for the English story of the critical ten years, 1549-1559. It is a story of violent extremes in the policies of successive all-powerful governments working on a people still Catholic, but so wrought by successive changes that all their certitudes were shaken.

[150]

The Lining Up for Battle: 1549-1559

Let us turn to the contemporary French interlude before the final struggle.

The importance of France, in the great struggle of the Reformation and its final effect, was this. France was, as usual, the battlefield. It was in France that the really heavy fighting was to be done, by great bodies of men under arms for thirty years.

Had France gone, one may say that, humanely speaking, the Catholic Church was doomed throughout Europe. The fact that in France the revolt was checked, and at last defeated—though not decisively so—maintained one large remaining remnant of Catholic unity in Europe and promoted the Catholic reaction later on in Germany. On the other hand, the fact that the revolt in France was not completely dominated, and that its adherents were not wholly wiped out, left the door open for the whole later rationalist movement and the political weakening of Catholicism in Europe from that time to our own.

The story of that great and critical war is too little known in English-speaking countries. It is of the first importance, in comprehending the results of the Reformation, to learn it on its largest lines. For while the Catholic Church was with difficulty uprooted in England by the organised action of a wealthy few who had seized all armed power and who tenaciously carried on their effort over a long lifetime and more, in France there was active combat between those who fiercely defended unity as essen-

tial to the healthy life of Europe and those who as
fiercely hated the Catholic Church in all its character.

In England there was a religious policy based on
the financial advantage of a few. There was but one
more popular rising in defence of the popular religion and no clash of regular armies. But in France
a duel was set in which the whole nation took part
under arms and upon the issue of which depended
the failure or survival of the Faith in the West.

There are three things which we must appreciate
about the French situation in these years preparatory
to open conflict, so far as France is concerned.

The first is that the French monarchy was a popular institution. It was representative of the whole
people of France, and particularly of the poor man
against the rich, of the weak man against the strong.
The French people being, like the mass of Europe at
that time, attached to the traditions of their past, the
monarchy was naturally the defender of the Catholic
Church against these new fierce efforts at disruption.

The second point is equally important. The
French monarchy and the now vivid and conscious
national life of the French people was in some peril
from the great power of the Emperor Charles V, who
ruled Germany and Spain at the beginning of these
ten years, and of his son Philip II at the end of them.
It was at issue, in other words, with Austria and
Spain. But Austria and Spain stood for Catholicism.
Charles V, the Emperor, who had been at the head
of both the German kingdom (a nominal kingdom,

in which his subordinates were more powerful than he) and of Spain, and of the Spanish conquests in the New World, and of the Netherlands, and of much of Italy, was, for all his political compromises, the obvious lay head of Catholic unity; his son, Philip II, was the resistance to the Reformation incarnate.

When Charles V abdicated, his brother Ferdinand became Emperor, holding the Austrian Arch-Duchy for his own, with only nominal power over other Germans. But Charles left his son Philip the Netherlands and Spain, and Franche-Comté, making a ring round France. Therefore the French monarchy in this critical period had an urgent and necessary political object: resistance to Charles V and after him to Philip II. But this necessary political object of the French Monarchy was in conflict with the religious instincts of the French people, upon which that Monarchy depended and which it represented.

For the religious instincts of the French Masses as of the English were for the traditional religion, and in Christendom as a whole Charles V, and later Philip II, were the champions of those instincts.

The result of this was that all during the lifetime of Francis I (up to his death in 1547), and again during the lifetime of his son Henry II (up to *his* death in 1559), the French monarchy was perpetually playing with the Reformation as a political factor: opposing it at home; defending it abroad.

Thus Wyatt's rebellion against Mary Tudor upon her accession was, as I have said, got up by the French

Ambassador because Mary (about to marry Philip, the son of Charles) would thereby be a weight against France in Europe. The attempt of Dudley (Northumberland) to make his daughter-in-law, Lady Jane Grey, Queen instead of Mary was also a French effort. No one can understand England at that moment unless he appreciates the fact that the French and Spanish influences were alternately predominant.

The third thing to appreciate is that John Calvin in making his counter-church and establishing his counter-Rome in Geneva was presenting an irresistible bait to the French squires and nobility: the bait of sacking religion in a country where religious endowments were very large.

This class had seen their fellows in North Germany and in England suddenly and hugely enriched by the loot of the Church and similar loot in France had been forbidden them.

Again, the Reformation meant for them greater independence from the Crown. They were still largely independent. Your average squire in France could exercise justice in his own village and the great nobles were still able to levy men for war, though not as directly as they had done in the past. On the top of that was the lure of the Reformation to scholar and humanist, that is, to those who wrote best and could most influence others. It was to the educated classes that the new movement appealed, as all new movements always appeal first to the educated classes. There was thus convergence of causes for the recruit-

ment of the wealthier people in France in favour of
the Reformation and against the national traditions.

Therefore it is that, when the conflict breaks out
later on, you find such a proportion of the leaders of
high French society on the anti-national and anti-
Catholic side. It is the exact opposite of what happened in England. In England the populace, which
detested the new break-up of society, could not find
leaders, from the Pilgrimage of Grace onwards, because the wealthier classes had had their fill of Church
land and other Church wealth, and knew that any
return to the national religion was perilous for them.
In France, on the other hand, the national feeling, the
popular tradition, though happily it found leaders,
had arrayed against it great bodies of the wealthier
classes, because, though they had not yet touched the
loot, they were expecting it.

Dominating all the French position in these ten
years of 1549-1559—the preparation for conflict—
still lies the great shadow of Calvin.

The influence of Calvin in these ten years began
to spread rapidly throughout the noble families,
which, after the Crown, were the natural leaders of
the French people. After 1559 you find a great mass
of their squires and more than half their very great
houses definitely joining the revolt against the Catholic Church, and how strong this movement was one
can best understand by two great examples of what
took place before 1559.

For in the ten years of which I am speaking, two

very great families, one of them royal, and soon to be heir to the throne, the other in the very highest positions of command, were got hold of by Calvin.

The first was the family of Bourbon. Anthony of Bourbon was King of Navarre; though only a distant cousin of the French King, Henry II, he was the presumptive heir to the throne, should Henry's sons fail to have issue. Those sons were very sickly; they did, in fact, fail to have issue; and therefore Anthony of Navarre's son, Henry, was the presumptive heir to the throne, within half a lifetime of Henry II's death, and ultimately became king as Henry IV.

Navarre's motive for joining, off and on, the religious revolt is quite clear. It strengthened him against the King. It is amusing to note that the poor fellow, like his son after him, found the puritanism of Geneva very irksome! He was perpetually giving scandal to the Saints! But anyhow, Calvin got hold of that family; it is a testimony to the political ability and fervour of the Genevan despot.

The Coligny example is equally interesting. The Colignys were important rich men of Burgundy, with a long lineage behind them; but the three brothers of this particular moment had an importance far greater than that of their ancestry, because they were the nephews of the Constable of Montmorency; Odet was made Cardinal; Andelot had great military commands; Gaspard was made Admiral of France. All three were got hold of by Cal-

vin in the period of which I speak; all three thought
it to their advantage to join the attack upon unity.
Ultimately the Cardinal was to appear quite openly
upon that side, to take a wife, and to fight against
the Catholic forces. Andelot, to whom Calvin wrote
his famous letter in 1558, was more vacillating, but
upon the whole secure for Calvin's side. As for Gaspard, the Admiral, he was much the most intelligent
and tenacious of the three brothers. He was exceedingly sly, played his cards carefully, and ended by
becoming the head of the new armed Calvinist movement among the French nobles.

The date, 1559, then is decisive. Observe how all
things converge towards it. It is in 1559 that the
first great religious revolt takes place in Scotland; it
is in 1559 that Henry II of France dies, leaving but
incompetent children, very young, and an embar-
rassed Queen Regent. It was immediately before,
that the Coligny family had been got hold of by
Calvin; it was immediately before, that Charles V
died; it was immediately before (in the November
of 1558), that Mary Tudor died, and William Cecil
with his new millionaires had brought in Elizabeth
as successor. It was in 1559 that for the first time a
full and powerful synod of the Calvinists in France
could meet in Paris, and did so. They got together
in May of that year and published their Confession
of Faith.

With 1559 ends the Preparation for Conflict.

How the Reformation Happened

Battle is about to be engaged. It was furious, it became universal. It ended in a draw. The Catholic Church was not destroyed, neither was European Unity restored.

CHAPTER V

The Universal Battle: 1559-1572

IN an attempt to answer the "Why" as well as the "How" of the Reformation, we have arrived well into the second half of its century, the sixteenth. It is 1559—over forty years since the first movements began.

All those who were in Power when the flood first poured, are dead: Charles the Emperor, Henry of England, Francis of France, Pope Leo.

The Generation which was active as young men in the original assault and defence is grown old and its effect has ceased. It has been replaced by a new body which cannot remember the old unquestioned Unity of Christendom.

The threat of cleavage—and of worse, of chaos in Europe—might have been dispelled and our people might have returned to their ancient security and happiness as they had returned so often before after similar perils, had not a convergence of ill-fortune and blunders come in to enhance the effects of fatal delay in Reform from within. At the very outset the Triumphant Turkish attack had paralysed the Emperor, political Rome had misunderstood the scale and character of the upheaval, Henry VIII had

[159]

blindly broken with it on a petty personal issue and had been led into the capital error of destroying the English Monasteries.

Thus the useful part of a lifetime had gone by with no remedy, with things getting worse and worse, men more and more accustomed to antagonism and falling more and more into two hostile bodies approaching war. The loot of the Church, when it had taken place, had had time to become a vested interest. Great groups had been brought up from childhood in the hatred of traditional doctrine and in enthusiasms of a new kind.

For ten years, as we have seen, from 1549 to 1559, these opposing camps had been marshalling for a live conflict. With 1559 the Universal battle opens. It rages with sudden changes of general victory and defeat for thirteen years—till 1572.

After that date its character changes: the probability of a decision one way or the other (a triumphal return of Catholicism, its obliteration) grows fainter. From twenty to thirty years more are spent in combat which is increasingly indecisive, each side consolidating its positions until its opponent cannot hope to drive them out, and the great affair ends without a decision. The Secession has succeeded in half Europe. The other half alone remains, exhausted, but saved for civilisation. The Catholic culture, wounded, henceforward on the defensive, constrained to stricter discipline because subject to continued pressure from without, is preserved, and Europe, though riven, is not destroyed.

This mighty combat of the first thirteen years is fought upon four sectors. The French, the English, the Scottish and that of the Netherlands. On the French the Battle is precariously won. On the English it is lost, but lost through the fortunes of the Scottish sector on the flank. In the Netherlands then is presented in miniature the character of the whole struggle: the checking of Spain in championship of the Faith: the successful succession of a northern minority: the division of the country into two cultures, Protestant and Catholic, as the whole of Europe was to be divided.

I will take these sectors in their order.

The French Sector

France in this mortal struggle of ideas was the Arena of Europe. In France where the affair was fought out with far more violence and with more changing fortunes than elsewhere the Huguenot lords and gentry opposed to the Catholic Church and to the ancient culture of their country very nearly won, but not quite. The fact that they *very nearly* won accounts for the long wrangle between opposing philosophies which has at once invigorated and disturbed the French for more than three hundred years. The fact that they did *not* win saved Catholicism in

Europe. If we consider the whole development, the French struggle covers nearly a century. Even if we only take it down to the last strictly religious fighting, the reduction of La Rochelle, it covers the whole of one very long lifetime. I deal here with the outset alone, from 1559 down to the day of St. Bartholomew in 1572.

Looking at the matter in its largest lines, what you have is this: the common people, here, as everywhere, strongly attached to their ancient religion, especially in Paris; the intellectuals divided, but—and this is essential—the nobility, i.e., the natural leaders and the fighting class, joining the attack upon Catholicism in a far larger proportion than any other section of the nation. There was a moment when quite one-half of the French squires, great and small, were in arms for the destruction of the Catholic Church, and of the most powerful and wealthiest, of the ducal families and their like, much more than half.

The main cause of this was the same as was at work all over Europe, the opportunity for loot.

The French nobility and gentry and chief merchants had looked on, hungry, while their fellows in England were being vastly enriched with the spoils of religion. Thus you get the paradoxical contrast between France and England at this moment: in England, because the squires were bulging with the recently purloined wealth of the Church, Catholic people could get only a few, or reluctant, or no military leaders to aid them against the unpopular clique which had seized the government; while in France the nation was almost lost to Catholicism by the armed effort of the disappointed squires who had not been able to get at that wealth.

Another subsidiary cause of the rebellious gentry's strength in France was the fact that after the death of Henry II in 1559 the French popular monarchy was suddenly badly weakened. Three boys were left to rule in succession, all of them wretchedly unhealthy, the last perverted, vicious and an offence, none of them capable of leaving children. Such an opportunity for rebellion was not to be missed by those who still retained so much of the old feudal independence. Perpetually in power (as Queen Mother) was the dowager Catherine de' Medici; an Italian, and, to many French nobles, an enemy. Then, again, the fact that Calvinism was a French thing, spread through the French language, bearing the marks of French order and intellectual discipline, had much to do with the strength of the Huguenot party, as had the widespread jealousy among their greater lords which was excited by the popularity, political power and towering wealth of the family of Lorraine, the head of which was the Duke of Guise.

This great soldier had retaken Calais from the English by a fine, rapid feat of arms, and the populace trusted to his continued victories against the foreigner or against rebels at home. There was no part of French life into which the family of Lorraine did not penetrate, yet they were in the French gentry's eyes

upstart, though of very ancient lineage, and among
their fellow nobles, in spite of marrying into the royal
blood, the family of Lorraine were hardly felt to be
French. They had not had two generations of
French life, and their origin was from the Empire.

What saved Catholicism in France was, in the first
place, the strong attachment of the people to the unbroken national monarchy, even when it had fallen
into such wretched hands as those of these three boys.
(I call them boys, for such they were when the
troubles began, the eldest only fifteen; but Henry
III, the last of them, did not die until he was over
forty.) What further helped was the intelligence of
Catherine de' Medici, who, no defender (or enemy)
of Catholic unity, piloted the monarchy most skil-
fully through the earlier part of this difficult passage
and thereby saved it. The period was like a duel between her and Calvin.

There was shock after shock. Hardly had the new
reigns of the young impotent kings begun when a
Huguenot conspiracy very nearly succeeded in seiz-
ing the person of the boy sovereign and upsetting
Guise. It is called The Tumult of Amboise. There
followed heavy fighting for two years between regular organised forces, and not till the battle of Dreux
was won by those who were defending the national
religion and the Crown did this episode end.

After a brief peace there was a second furious bout
of fighting, within a year. The whole situation is
exceedingly confused, because nobles and princes

changed allegiance continually, now for the monarchy, now against it, according as they saw greater chance of money-getting on one side or the other.

The parties are not defined. The same individual, the heir apparent to the throne, Anthony of Bourbon, King of Navarre, for example, was, as has been said, a recruit of Calvin's. Yet he vacillates. He will appear now as Catholic and now as Huguenot. The Coligny family, though the most prominent on the Huguenot side, makes its peace over and over again with the King, or rather with the Court, and the slyest and most intelligent of the three Coligny brothers, the Admiral, with such great forces at his command, actually, at a last reconciliation, accepts the revenues of an Abbey offered him by the Queen Mother.

Though the Huguenots were at first defeated in the field, and though the populace had begun to reply to their massacres and destruction of churches, shrines and private houses by counter-massacres, yet there was a moment when it looked as though the rebel nobility would win. The circumstances under which their attempt failed produced what is called "The St. Bartholomew." Its circumstances were as follows:—

The vacillating King of Navarre had for wife the heiress of the family of Albret, the great lords of all that district in Gascony which lies east of the Landes, under the Pyrenees. Her name was Joan, and she was inflamed with a peculiar, personal, passionate hatred of the Catholic Church. In 1569, three years before the critical moment, when it looked as though the rebel Huguenot nobles would be able to capture the French Crown and dissolve the State, her Huguenot general in the South had accepted the surrender of the Catholic nobility under a promise that their lives should be spared. In spite of that pledge he (and Joan) had them massacred in cold blood upon St. Bartholomew's Day.

This was the first Massacre of St. Bartholomew.

The date was not forgotten. Three years later, in 1572, her son, Henry of Navarre, now grown to manhood, was to be married to his cousin, the daughter of the Queen Mother, the sister of the King of France. The marriage was to take place at Paris.

Coligny was there, keeping his false truce with the Queen Mother who was in terror of his strength and, as falsely as himself, concealed her hatred. If he maintained his leadership her son's crown was lost. Here then was Coligny in Paris on that critical date in the history of France and Europe, patently at the head of the rebels and growing mightily in power, with great influence over the young king and apparently upon the point of taking all the forces of the country into his own hands. In Coligny was incarnate the rebellion of the nobles and their menace to the Crown. He and his were on the eve of winning.

For the marriage of the young heir of Navarre, who was later to be King Henry IV, and who was not only heir apparent to the French Throne but much the most prominent figure on the Protestant side, a very great number of the Huguenot squires, great and little, had poured into Paris, all armed, of course, and all the greater ones with a considerable retinue of fighting men.

What followed was a mixture of three things: a determination of young Guise to be avenged for the death of his great father, murdered by the Huguenots under Coligny's direction; a deliberate plan laid by Catherine de' Medici, the Queen Mother, to save her son and herself from the tyranny of Coligny, and— far the most important factor—an outburst of popular fury against the Huguenot nobles. According to which of these three elements in the affair we emphasise do we produce one or the other of the many false versions of that famous night. We must give them their just proportions to write just history. The massacre of St. Bartholomew might have taken place without the action of Guise or even perhaps of the Queen Mother, Catherine de' Medici. It certainly could not have taken place but for the intense feeling of the people of Paris and the people of France in general against the anti-national and anti-Catholic attitude of their nobles.

There had already been one attempt upon the life of Coligny; it had failed, though he had been wounded. A second was made, almost certainly by the orders of young Guise, upon the Eve of the Feast of St. Bartholomew, the 24th of August, 1572. Assassins were despatched to Coligny's house, where he lay recovering from his wound. Young Guise, the son and heir of the murdered chief of the Catholic party, waited outside the house until the Admiral was despatched and his body thrown from the window. Then followed an attack by armed men of the Guise faction on the Huguenot nobles in the city, but the decisive thing was that, at the inception of this partial and restricted faction-fight the whole populace joined in. It was the populace who were the main agents of the affair.

There had been any amount of massacring and killing up and down the country for more than ten years, and the emphasis commonly laid by anti-Catholic historians upon this particular popular outbreak is unhistorical. Moreover, we do not know the total number of victims in Paris and the other towns, where further massacres followed. They have been put at a few hundreds; they have been put at many thousands. Perhaps about two thousand is the right figure: we shall never know. What is important to remember upon St. Bartholomew is this: that for a time it thoroughly cowed the anti-Catholic nobles. The fury of the populace had a lasting effect which could never be undone.

Their passionate deed did not end the civil war by any means; on the contrary, the memory of the massacre made those wars, when they began again, more bitter than ever. But it was clear after this year, 1572, that the rich Huguenot squires and lords could never destroy the Crown; and that the general traditions of the French national culture were saved. Therefore, while one must guard oneself against the error of making the Massacre exceptional in the story of the time (all the religious wars in Europe, from the Pilgrimage of Grace to the abominations of Cromwell in Ireland are one long series of wholesale slaughterings), yet one may well take its year, 1572, not only as the end of the first period of the great French religious civil wars, but as the date after which the destruction of the French monarchy and national religion is impossible.

The English Sector

Mary Tudor had died at the very end of the year 1558. There followed an unbroken succession of governments in England which for two long lifetimes—to 1685—had it for their permanent, tenacious, unswerving object to extirpate what had been the national religion.

It was a very slow process. The tyranny worked for fifty years upon a people which, from almost wholly Catholic in general ideas, tradition, and sympathy, it turned to being about half and half; in the next fifty anti-Catholic governments, with the majority of the nation now behind them, worked upon a still very large though steadily decreasing Catholic minority.

This policy of completely uprooting the Catholic

[169]

Church from English soil succeeded. It succeeded mainly through the negative instrument of forbidding all action which could keep the Catholic Church alive: preventing children from receiving a knowledge of Catholic truth, hunting out the priesthood till this was reduced to a handful of wandering, concealed men in peril of their lives. But the capital agent of the change was the stamping out of the Mass.

As we approach this long story, there is one thing always to be borne in mind: that the history of it as taught in our schools and universities is an official story and a thoroughly false one. Whether it be to the advantage of the State that official history alone should be taught, and that a criticism of it should be unknown, may be debated. There are those who think that such legends strengthen a nation. Others (and I am one) think that historical falsehood weakens a nation.

Be that as it may, the history we are asked to accept in the English tongue upon the English side of the Reformation at least (and a great part of the Continental side as well) is no more than propaganda. To read it one would imagine that Burghley's England was a Protestant nation with an especially pronounced anti-Catholic twist; that in the midst of such an imaginary English people there survived a few unnational, exceptional people whom it was necessary for the sake of national survival to destroy. The truth is exactly the other way.

The mass of England was Catholic in tradition and

feeling during all the last half of the sixteenth century. Even into the beginning of the seventeenth the tradition survived. A good half of the people still had Catholic sympathies in the earlier years of James I. A quarter of them had in varying degrees Catholic sympathies (and half that quarter was willing to sacrifice heavily for the sake of openly confessing Catholicism) as late as the fall of the Stuarts in 1685-1688. But during the whole time the steady official persecuting pressure continued; the practice of a Catholic life was rendered impossible, and what had once been the normal open profession of the national tradition in religious things fell to being but a sentiment, and then, from a sentiment to being but a memory, and at last, after 1688, died out.

Let us appreciate, to begin with, the essential fact that the age 1559-1572 was not "Elizabethan." Elizabeth Tudor was not a great Queen leading all England in a triumphant march towards a new and larger destiny; she was the figure-head of a new Plutocracy, the men who had made vast fortunes out of raiding the Church, who kept up for years a suppressed civil war lest the return of Catholicism should ruin them, and under whose unpopular oppression wealth and population declined. Some of them were what we to-day call millionaires, a much larger number were men of smaller but substantial fortune swelled with Church loot, and the "tail" was a whole army of people who had speculated in that loot, sold and resold it, and retained sundry fragments.

At the head of this vested interest was William Cecil, later created Lord Burghley, whose first steps in power I have already mentioned. I have also given the sources of that power. William Cecil was the most industrious and the most intelligent of them all; he thought more clearly; he concentrated more thoroughly and continuously. His family became the chiefs of the new dominating class, spoke for them and stood for them, from the moment he put Elizabeth upon the throne to his death, when his son Robert carried on till long after Elizabeth's reign. The period of uprooting Catholicism in England, fifty years and more, was indeed, "the period of the Cecils" rather than of Elizabeth, but it must be always borne in mind that the Cecils, father and son, were but the leaders and the spokesmen, and most intelligent organisers, of a new great vested interest. They would have been nothing but for the economic revolution produced by the seizure of clerical endowments under Henry VIII and his brother-in-law, Seymour, and the rest between 1536 and 1553.

William Cecil advanced to the headship of English Government (in a day when government was absolute) by three qualities which he possessed in a superior degree—industry, clarity of thought, and devotion to one object:—money.

As secretary to the All-powerful Council when Henry VIII died, William Cecil was the only one in that gang who did serious work. He saw and filed and kept all the papers. He in obscurity "ran the show," while the other members, especially the Seymours, the King's brothers-in-law, and their hangers-on, neglected business, and wallowed in their immense new-found wealth.

When Dudley, who had got himself made Duke of Northumberland by his fellow looters, wanted to destroy Somerset, the head of the Seymours, he had, as we saw, to turn to the indispensable William Cecil for aid.

Cecil alone had all the records of everybody's doings; Cecil by the betrayal of his master, Seymour, sprang from being a man of moderate fortune—what we should call to-day three or four thousand a year—to a financial position which put him in the very centre of the New Millionaires. He became one of them himself, and the most important.

After the great popular rising which introduced Mary Tudor he lay low. He had backed the French plot for Lady Jane Grey, and lied freely about it afterwards to save his skin; but Mary was afraid to touch him in any case, and as he was certainly devoid of any religious feeling on either side, like most of that wealthy clique, he did himself no violence by manifesting Catholic devotion so long as Mary lived. He bided his time; he knew that the Tudors were diseased and short-lived (later on, as we shall see, a miscalculation on that point led his clique to murder Mary Stuart).

At Mary's death he introduced Elizabeth for the throne with great ease. For though she was vaguely attached by upbringing to the unpopular "reform-ing" minority, she was of the family to which the English were now used as monarchs.

The legitimate heir to the English throne at this moment (winter of 1558-1559) was Elizabeth's cousin, Mary Stuart, Queen of Scotland and married to the Boy-King of France, for Elizabeth herself was a bastard, not only in the eyes of Europe as the daughter of the Boleyn woman and born while her father's true wife was still alive, but even by the law which Henry himself had made and which declared his so-called marriage with Anne null and void.

It was the young Queen of Scots' rightful claim to the English throne which makes the story of the time turn in Scotland.

But the Scottish native was at that time not only alien but enemy to the English mind.

However Elizabeth was on the spot. That she was alive at all was due to the impolitic mercy of her elder, and legitimate, half-sister.

Mary Tudor was advised to put her to death after Wyatt's rebellion to which her name was attached, but she listened to the plea of Philip of Spain, to whom she was devoted, and that plea had saved Elizabeth's life.

There then was Elizabeth on the throne by Cecil's action, making Mary a convenient accepted figurehead for the new financial interests which Cecil represented.

During the whole of her long reign (it lasted close

on half a century) this unfortunate woman was never free.

She had no real sympathy with the growing Protestant cause upon the Continent. The rebellion against monarchical authority, which was the very essence of it in Scotland, Germany, the Netherlands and France, was odious to her. The idea of a married clergy was repulsive to her. All her instincts were with the general culture of Europe: she was herself a widely cultivated woman and fanatical enthusiasms are odious to such. Moreover, she loved popularity, and she knew that the people over whom she was set were in the bulk attached to the national tradition in religion.

But she was not free. It was the prime business of the New Millionaires, with Cecil at their head, to root out the Catholic Church; and after more than half a century of work the corner was turned. Before the end of the first quarter of the seventeenth century the majority of England had been made anti-Catholic. Their successors completed the task. In the last half of the seventeenth century the mass of England was anti-Catholic. Sixteen hundred and eighty-eight was the death blow. During the eighteenth century the Catholic faith of the English disappeared.[1]

The first ten or twelve years of the affair are the critical ones. Cecil and his lot, firmly in power, began to act in early 1559. The process was so grad-

[1] The Catholic Body dwindled to less than one per cent.

ual and so subtle that for ten years there was no considerable uprising on any part of the English people against novelties that irked them. When that uprising took place—in 1570—it was but partial and was suppressed with the utmost barbarity—a repression coming opportunely for the new governing power. At the same time came the solemn denunciation of the English Government in the person of Elizabeth, its legal head, by the Pope of the day. That gave Cecil the opportunity for acting as he could not have acted ten years before, and for beginning a process of making all practice of the Catholic Faith from exceedingly difficult as it had been until that moment, impossible. When the popular rising in favour of the Faith had been put out in blood, Cecil was in greater power than ever. He became Lord Burghley, and we may take here, as in France, the year 1572, after his new title and with the last embers of rebellion grown cold, as the turning-point.

We have, then, in the English story, to consider the years 1559 to 1572 as a preparatory period in which all was made ready for the uprooting of the Catholic Faith among Englishmen but during which it was necessary for the plotters to go slowly.

During the whole of these first years, before the rebellion, no one was put to death for treason on the ground of religion. The Mass was abolished, of course, and, on the principle of striking at the heads of society, those of the governing class who remained Catholic were outrageously fined if they failed to conform to the new rites. But Cecil and his group were careful not to be definite in doctrine. They framed the vaguest articles of religion compatible with the getting rid of the Mass and of Catholic practice. At the beginning of the process they winked, with hypocritical purpose of slowly "letting down" tenacious customs, at much private practice of the religion they designed to destroy. Priests sometimes said Mass and often enough gave Catholic communion after reading the new official service, and at first the odd custom was condoned. Cecil was careful not to administer the Oath of Supremacy to more people than was absolutely necessary; he left the bulk of the clergy undisturbed, and though the Government had to set up a new hierarchy as best they could, yet they took immense pains to get some sort of mechanical continuity, and did in fact achieve this. The new Bishops whom Elizabeth herself so heartily despised, though ordained with Calvinistic rites, could say that each had suffered or enjoyed the laying on of hands by some other who, in his turn, had suffered or enjoyed the same from a member of the old episcopacy.

Meanwhile the opportunity for further loot arose. The new hierarchy was roundly shorn of the incomes the old had enjoyed, and the difference was pocketed by the gang in power. But no blood was shed, and the laity were in great measure unmolested.

There was thus fostered an enduring illusion during these ten years that a reconciliation might take place. The illusion was entertained both at home and abroad, though it must have made Cecil smile. The English Government was asked to send representatives to the Council of Trent; and the Pope perhaps expected them to come. Elizabeth herself, I think, shared in that illusion: at any rate, in private she spoke of how slight a line, what unimportant details, divided her from orthodoxy.

But the directing power of the time was not to be baffled. The English situation was clinched by the much more violent and conclusive Scottish movement. What firmly established Cecil's plan was the capture of Scotland by English influence, and its consequences in the imprisonment and death of the Scottish Queen.

The Scottish Sector

Scotland at this time was of less account than to-day in comparing population. It was one of the smallest kingdoms in Europe as to numbers, and thought of as something remote upon the edges of the known world.

Yet it had a particular place for learning and for character, but most of all for this: that the nation had successfully withstood English power and was an important ally, on the further side of England, for any continental power opposed to the English Government of the day: and therefore, generation after generation, the ally of France.

It was far less strong than England. The two

countries stood in population perhaps as one to four, in fighting power the balance was more even, but in wealth less. Scotland was poor, even for her extent. She had barely a quarter of England's arable area, she had far less than a quarter of England's total wealth. Next we must again recall that in 1559, to the average Scot, England was still—as she had been for centuries—the enemy country. Here more than in any other department of Reformation history, we must beware of reading the present into the past.

Scotland had achieved national independence at a higher price than any other country in Europe, and had confirmed that independence precisely in those three generations when separate national feeling was everywhere growing in consciousness. The English Crown had claimed Feudal supremacy over Scotland throughout the Middle Ages, and nothing had defeated that very tenable claim but the determination of the Scottish people to resist. Leaders might yield; but the lesser gentry and their followers and the mass of the people perpetually returned to the charge. The small fertile belt of country, between Forth and Clyde, was harried over and over again by English invading hosts far stronger than any possible defence. Yet the position was always ultimately retrieved.

The Reformation it was which put an end—slowly —to this ancient habit of mind. It began by dissolving the ancient alliance of Scotland with France. It concluded under a common monarch, and—what was far more important—under a common moral system. For in spite of the long and fierce conflict between Calvinism and the official English establishment, an essential unity of ethical principles spread throughout Britain. What we call to-day the Protestant Culture became common to both nations and welded them. What we call the Catholic Culture, the ancient maker of each, became abhorrent to both.

Next let it be noted that Scotland had suffered from a quite exceptional run of bad luck in the matter of monarchy, which was the vital social principle of the Middle Ages and the core of the nations developing therefrom.

There had been a succession of children coming to the throne, with that inevitable consequence of minorities, potential or actual rebellion against the Crown.

This weakness went back to the very heart of the Middle Ages. After Robert the Bruce came a child, who later, as king, had no strength. Then, after two old men, only ten years or so of strong government; then a couple of lengthy periods in which the monarch was again a child; then eleven years of what was virtually civil war between the king and a great feudal house—and so on. There had been a moment of real national monarchy under James IV (Henry VIII's brother-in-law and elder contemporary); had it continued, all might have been well. But James was killed at Flodden, when he was only just over forty years of age. Again a child was left on the throne. That child in his turn, James V, dying just after the defeat of the Solway when he was barely thirty, again left a baby on the throne—the baby who was to be Mary Queen of Scots.

In a period of two centuries and a half, there was minority after minority, and in all that space of years nothing like a lifetime of strong ordered rule.

On account of this national tradition the nobles—everywhere in Europe such a threat to the throne—and especially the nobles connected with the royal blood, were inordinately powerful.

Now the dominating factor in the mid-sixteenth century of Scotland, after so many misfortunes, was the treble situation of the Church.

I say "treble" because the three parts of it, though mutually dependent, are distinct.

First, there was the fact that the clerical wealth was extravagantly large. In this small and, at that time, exceptionally poor, country a Papal delegate, observing the conditions and reporting as accurately as he could to the Apostolic See, said that by the end of the Middle Ages one-half of what he called the "wealth of the country" went to ecclesiastical revenues.

Here, as in the case of England, we must understand, of course, by the "wealth of the country" not the total wealth, but the surplus rents payable to the Lords of the Manors and of Towns, after the livelihood of the populace had been provided for. It may roughly be compared to the wealth not of modern England as a whole, but of the people who pay tax on unearned income. Even so, to have one-half in the hands of the clerics was an overwhelming proportion, unnatural and exasperating. The highest proportion of Clerical to other Manorial incomes estimated for England over the Border was a third, and, as I have said on a previous page, that estimate was certainly exaggerated. In Scotland, even if the Papal delegate's estimate was exaggerated, it was clearly far larger.

The second factor in the Scottish position was the corruption of the Church, which, very bad everywhere throughout Europe in the fifteenth century, had in Scotland reached a degree hardly known elsewhere. That is why the true explanation of the Scottish anti-Catholic movement, its crimes and enthusiasms, is not that the Scottish people suddenly became aflame with devotion to Calvin's theology, but that against the small minority which originally was so inflamed, the vast majority remained indifferent. No considerable body in Scotland was concerned to suffer for the Faith; but many individuals were ready to die in battle or even in torment to express their hatred of the Church. There were few provinces of Europe, no independent realm, where the practice of religion, in the Lowlands at least, had so sunk. There was no great popular insurrection in Scotland against the Decatholicising of the country by the rich, as there were abortive, though violent, risings in England, successful ones in France.

Thirdly, the gross abuse of lay encroachment upon

Church revenues, of using Church revenues as mere income producers for the bastards or cadets of the great families, had proceeded farther in Scotland than in any other part of Western Christendom.

It is astonishing to note to-day, when we are rid of it, how deeply that cancer had then bitten in. We have seen how bad it was in France when the Guises could, in the very heart of the Reformation, and as a sort of challenge to the Reformers, make a young boy of their family, a lad of fourteen, Archbishop of Rheims and also Abbot of three of the most important monasteries in France. But in Scotland things were far worse. Apart from the general corruption of the clergy, and the irregularity of the great monasteries (following upon their wealth) there was the handing over of the revenues of episcopal sees and monastic endowments to the sons of the great families. Whether they were technically laymen or clerics made very little difference. The holding of religious funds had become a mere provision of income for royalties and nobles. James V had so endowed three of his bastards, who were given Kelso, Melrose, Holyrood, and St. Andrews; and this is only one high example out of a score.

Nevertheless, though they had already (unlike the English gentry) taken a large part of clerical revenue *before* the Reformation, it was greatly to the advantage of the Scottish nobles to accept the Reformation movement, and they leapt at that advantage.

The Crown had for long been held with difficulty

against the great families. Many of those families were descended from Kings and could attempt the succession against a young girl, married abroad and under foreign protection. To those of the Royal blood the Calvinistic Movement offered chances of supplanting this Catholic heiress to the Throne. To all who were already drawing some part of clerical revenue, it offered an easy path for absorbing the whole.

The Scottish attack upon the official Church which broke out with such violence in the middle of the sixteenth century was not a movement. It was not general. Still less was it universal. But, on the other hand, it was not met, as in France, by any general, national counter-attack. It was permitted and engineered by a corrupt group of nobles who used it for wealth and power. It was driven by the force of intense Calvinism in some few, of indignation in many, followed by a rabble with adventurers ready for pay and plunder on either side. That it certainly was not.

The Scottish Movement began as the assault on the official and decayed clerical organism of a frenzied minority which grew rapidly greater, and which had opposed to it no serious resistance among the masses. Its determining conditions were the exceptional corruption of the Church and the power and avarice of the great nobles, in whose hands was everything: for the crown had weakened to tottering.

Historians have represented the Calvinist revolution of 1559 as a movement essentially popular, with John Knox at its head. It was nothing of the kind. It was a movement mainly aristocratic, using the hardly sane excitement of Knox and his (at first) comparatively few followers. Their leaders feared no solid resistance from the bulk of society, still less from an executive which had lost its powers.

Mary Stuart, later, for a moment, Queen of France and legitimate heiress to England, had been left as nominal queen of Scotland, a baby, after the death of her father James V (1542). Thenceforward every effort was made by the English Government to capture Scotland. This policy had many roots. There was the old idea of making Scotland subject to England—the one thing which provoked every Scotchman to fury. There was the anxiety of Henry VIII not to have a Papal country on his flank after he had broken with the Pope. There was the still greater anxiety of Henry's brothers-in-law, the Seymours, in the midst of their raking in Church property after Henry's death in 1547, not to have a Catholic country beyond the Border supporting the strongly Catholic tradition of the English people.

The first proposition was to affiance the Baby Mary Stuart to the child Edward Tudor, heir to Henry. It was backed by Henry's own heavy bribery and intrigue among the mutually jealous and all-powerful Scottish nobles. It failed. Mary Stuart was married to the son of the French King, and the French alliance against England was re-affirmed.

But that French alliance with Scotland in the days when little Edward Tudor was nominally King, and later, when his half-sister, Mary Tudor, was really Queen of England, did not succeed. The new reforming movement in Scotland was opposed to it because the Queen Mother, who was regent, James V's widow, was a Guise; that is, of the family which were leading the Catholic national movement in France against the Huguenots. Further, the French troops in Scotland, brought in to support the Queen Mother as Regent were unpopular. The spirit of nationalism was already so strong that their foreignness was an offence. After he had put Elizabeth on the throne, Cecil threw all the weight of the English Government on to the rebel side in Scotland. From that moment onward proceeded a development of events whereby the hold of the English Crown over Scotland became stronger and stronger through the progress of the Reformation.

The anti-Catholic camarilla which had hold of government in England acquired control over Scotland, ultimately, by way of division among the Scottish people and by their steady support for the most active and enthusiastic faction among them—the Reformers.

The Queen Regent of Scotland could not really govern; her nobles were too strong for her. The most important and powerful of the gentry saw their opportunity for loot here as their brethren had seen it throughout Europe, and they leagued themselves for an attack upon the Church.

The decisive year was the same as the year of Elizabeth's accession, 1559; and in the next year, 1560, there was a violent outbreak of burning and destruction of churches, smashing of images and windows, robbery of valuables of every kind, comparable to the later outbreak in Holland; and there was no government in Scotland strong enough to suppress that anarchy, for it had the greedy nobles behind it. Shortly afterwards Mary, the young Queen, strongly Catholic by upbringing, the widow of a Catholic boy-king of France, herself only nineteen, came back to exercise nominal rule in this disturbed land, which was really in the hands of the great landed families —and these determined upon the ruin of the Church.

She came back in 1561; she fell in 1567. The story of those feverish six years has been written upon every conceivable surmise, for there is so much in it that is mysterious and can never be solved, so much that depends upon our right reading of hidden personal motive, that there will always remain a large margin of doubt upon individual acts and intentions of Mary's.

But the main fact is clear enough. The marvel is not that this high-spirited, courageous and finely athletic young woman, should have succumbed; the marvel is that she should have maintained some kind of royal position so long.

The young widow was re-married by English influence to a refugee at the English court, the cretinous, diseased, and vicious boy, her cousin Darnley I—himself a claimant to the throne of Scotland, had he not also now claimed the crown matrimonial. This impossible young fellow was not only the natural victim of Mary's other relatives (who each nursed his own hopes to reach the throne), but also bitterly offended the men of greatest influence around him.

He was found dead after an explosion, which shattered a part of the house in which he had lain the night before. It was not the explosion that killed him; he was found strangled.

Already the Scottish nobles in revolt, pensioners of the English Crown, had killed Mary's secretary, who was also—probably without justice—called her lover. She was accused of complicity in the murder of Darnley, whom she had come to loathe; she married —with Protestant rites—a man far more deeply implicated in the murder, one of the great Protestant nobles, Bothwell. Yet the rising that followed was provoked, so far as the town mobs were concerned, much more by her religion than by accusations against her morals; so far as the nobles were concerned that opposition was provoked by the obvious opportunity offered by her defencelessness for their own enrichment. Their revolt succeeded. The rebellious lords took Mary prisoner. She escaped, lost her last battle, and fled to England to receive aid there against the rich men who henceforward had Scotland in their hands, and who had at their head her own half-brother, now Regent. Cecil had shepherded all this. Her flight was decisive, for to have Mary Stuart thus in England was Cecil's great opportunity.

Elizabeth would have saved her and helped her; but Elizabeth did not govern England; Cecil governed England. He had already provoked and sustained the rebellion in Scotland; he now saw to it that the unfortunate refugee queen should be gradually turned into a prisoner, and held fast while his work beyond the border was completed. Mary had left in Scotland a baby, the son of Darnley, who was to grow up to be James VI of that country and James I of England. As the result of Cecil's success he was bred to Calvinism.

Mary Stuart had fled to England in the year 1567. For two years, though virtually a prisoner, she was, in appearance, free, with (at first) something like a court in exile, receiving openly; but long before those two years were over it was clear from Cecil's policy that, unless she and her friends took action, Mary would lose her freedom; for she was not only by legitimate descent rightful Queen of England, but also, now, the national rallying point of the large Catholic majority in England.

When she found herself a prisoner she appealed to Elizabeth. But the governing clique would not allow her to see Elizabeth—on the excuse that certain documents (the Casket Letters, known to-day to be forged) proved her complicity in Darnley's murder.

Mary Stuart was in the toils. Elizabeth herself, inclined to support a sovereign against rebels, feared to strengthen the legitimate Heiress to England—for Elizabeth, though compelled to it by the will of others, had one fixed passion coinciding with theirs —to retain the Throne on which these others maintained her, and by whose favour she wore the Crown.

But even had Elizabeth still wished to receive and help Mary, her masters would not have allowed it. Without action Mary was doomed.

Action therefore was taken. A vigorous effort was made for the restoration of the older state of things in England, or at any rate for an approach to it—at the very least for the ousting of Cecil. The Duke of Norfolk was proposed as a husband for Mary Stuart, and a considerable group—some of them drawn from the older nobility—supported the attempt to get rid of Cecil.

They failed. They had behind them without a doubt the mass of opinion in England in their opposition to Cecil and their aim at restoring the national tradition in religion. They had not the same backing for a foreign queen and the ousting of a Tudor. The effort failed. This effort against Cecil having failed, the consequences of its failure were these: First of all a violent revolt of the English people in the North against the destruction of the Mass and of all their social and religious traditions. It had two successive phases, and was crushed with an appalling severity; the populace were butchered in hundreds and there

was not a village that had not its corpses swinging
from the trees. And this was the last upheaval of the
English populace against any of their governors. It
was the last of the great English popular movements
against the Reformation.

Next, or coincidently, came the action of the Pope,
Pius V, disapproved of by every prince in Europe,
which released Elizabeth's subjects from their oath of
allegiance (the revolt was in 1569 and 1570—the
Pope's Bull was not promulgated till the early days
of 1570, but prepared late in 1569). Cecil, having
now governed for ten years, hitherto able to boast
that no man had been put to death for his religion or
even for treason until the great rebellion, having imposed the new Protestant Liturgy upon an unwilling
people, having set up, and kept under his thumb, a
definitely Protestant régime in Scotland, and holding
Mary Stuart a prisoner, had finally triumphed. He
becomes Lord Burghley, the title by which he is
known to history, in 1571. By the next year, 1572,
all danger to him is over; the Pope's action has given
Cecil his excuse for vigorous action against the leaders
of the Catholic majority, and the policy of gradually
extirpating the traditional religion of the English
from the English mind is firmly in the saddle.

We may take this date, 1572, and say that it marks
the moment whenceforward England through the
success of Cecil's intrigue with the Scottish nobles
and his suppression of the great Catholic rebellion will
probably cease to recover the Faith, while France,

after the explosion of popular fury in the St. Bartholomew in the same year, will certainly not be Huguenot, and yet as certainly, seeing the strength of the
Huguenot nobles, will never again be homogeneously
Catholic.

The Netherlands Sector

In the many factors which combined both to produce that confusion of Europe called the Reformation and to confirm and make permanent its ultimate
results in the seventeenth century, the struggle in the
Netherlands holds a place of its own.

It was the chief cause of decline in Spanish power,
or at any rate the chief cause of that decline's coming
so rapidly; and Spanish power was the support of
tradition and of European unity at the moment when
the troubles of that Power in the Netherlands began.

Again, the struggle in the Netherlands furnished
a model profoundly affecting England; it suggested
the use of sea-power against the gravely insufficient
sea-power of the South. What was far more important, it showed the way to set up government by
the rich and destroy popular monarchy. It also
showed how national and provincial councils (there
called "Estates," here called "Parliament"), could be
used as an instrument of the popular monarchy.

Again the wars of the Dutch against their Spanish
King showed how the strength of a Commonwealth
may be founded upon commerce.

Above all, that successful rebellion confirmed the

then anarchic assertion that the local interest of one society might assert itself against the common interests of Europe.

In all these things the Netherlands led the way, and were an example which the forces counterpart to them in Britain instinctively followed. It was on the model of the Dutch that the English pitted Parliament against the Crown: made commerce a new foundation for national wealth: learnt how shipping could control Continental military supply. The Dutch influence upon England remained throughout the seventeenth century, until at last the English religious quarrel was finally settled—as some believe forever—by a Dutch invasion financed with Dutch money, and having at its head a Dutch usurping claimant to the English throne (William III), who, though set up by the organised wealth of the great squires and merchants of this country, and though in his own culture and manner French, drew his position from the headship of the great Netherland House of Orange.

The main points to keep well in mind, and to the foreground in any attempt to understand the key struggle in the Netherlands, are as follows:

(1) The origin of the trouble was economic, not religious. A foolish and intolerable tax unsuited to the conditions of these mercantile towns was the main cause of the original revolt. The religious factor was at first a secondary matter. It increased as the struggle proceeded, after the same fashion as it

grew to importance during the Great Rebellion in England—which was largely the reflection of Dutch action a lifetime before.

The religious factor, indeed, saved all that could be saved for Spain. But for it, Spain would have lost the whole of the Netherlands. All the Netherlands disliked the blunders of Spanish Government and were ready to fight it when they could not get redress; but when the Calvinist merchants in the north mixed the thing up with an attack on the popular religion, the general rebellion failed: most of the provinces in the Netherlands defended their religion. It was Catholic disgust with Calvinism which, in spite of strong provincial patriotism and dislike of Spanish rule, kept the Southern Netherlands in touch with Europe, and gave us the Catholic culture of what we call to-day Belgium.

(2) Here, as everywhere in the history of the Reformation, but more perhaps than in other departments of that history, we have to beware of reading history backwards. We must not think of a Dutch nation nobly struggling to be free from wicked Spanish oppressors, and all the rest of it. There was no Dutch nation. There was a fairly homogeneous local provincial culture common to all those wealthy cities from the Artois to the lower Rhine; that is, from a district including Valenciennes, Lille, Dunkirk, Arras to the south, to the northern shores of Friesland, and including Groningen and Gelderland to the northeast.

To all the rich self-governing towns of that region (to-day split up into Belgium, Holland, and a strip of northern France), the Spanish King was not an alien power, nor regarded by the Netherland cities as a foreign tyrant. He was the lawful sovereign of all the Low Countries, long accepted as such, even after the struggle had begun, and the complaint of the Netherlands was continued for years together *not* against King Philip as King, but against his advisers and policy.

It was only after years of sporadic civil war that a section among these Lowlanders, and only a section, desired separation from what was called in the language of the time its "natural Prince."

(3) Even that lesser part of the Netherlands which made a religious affair of the struggle against Spain, and established itself as the United Provinces (in modern English "Holland") would not have succeeded had not the New Millionaires in England, with the Cecils at their head, given them secret but full support in spite of their figurehead, the unfortunate Elizabeth, who detested the idea of supporting rebels, but in this, as in all else of essential policy, had to submit. This open support given to the Dutch at the end of the first acute phase, when Cecil sent over troops, was less than useless. It made things worse for the Dutch merchants instead of better. The silly Leicester was beaten flat by Spanish military power. But secret support of the rebellion went on for years, from almost the beginning of Cecil's dom-

ination over England, and it was of continuous value to the rebels. It was the interference with supplies (especially the keeping back of Spanish money sent to pay the Spanish troops, when the supply ships running before a storm, had taken refuge for a time in an English harbour) and the permanent threat that such secret support might materialise into open support, which most heavily handicapped the ill-considered efforts of Philip II, lawful King of the Netherlands. But by the time this open support appeared, the necessity imposed upon that king of turning round to fight a new front against France had rendered impossible a complete Spanish victory.

We must remember throughout that the rebel movement in the Netherlands was essentially oligarchic. It was the work not, at first, of the people but of a small powerful group. One can hardly call it aristocratic, for the rich men who led it were in the main commercial; but the whole life and soul of it was the insistence, in a wealthy class, upon what the more enthusiastic believed to be their rights, and what all knew to be certainly to their material advantage.

This wealthy oligarchy of the Netherlands towns was supported at first by the bulk of provincial and local feeling, though vaguely and confusedly; but as the struggle went on the popular masses were less and less to be relied upon, and it was the rich men who carried the thing through in their own interests. Though the House of Orange, which was the original traitor of the Royal cause (after receiving innumer-

able benefits from the Crown which they betrayed),
stands there permanent in the whole history, its character is not that of a rival monarchy to Spain: it is
but one of the most important in a set of millionaire
interests, though special value was lent to that house
by the tenacious character of its chiefs, notably that
of the original elder William, somewhat ridiculously
nick-named "The Silent." [2]

I call the story a falsehood without hesitation, because there is no evidence of it, except that advanced
by William himself *twenty-one* years later; he himself is our only witness, and, even so, we hear nothing
of it for half a lifetime after it was supposed to have
happened. Payen's story can only have come from
William himself. There are no witnesses; and the
only other person concerned, Henry II, died immediately after the supposed interview.

Lastly, no one will believe that a man of the years
and position of the King of France at the time would
have made a *sole* confidant of a young fellow such as
William of Orange at that moment was, and one who
had been brought up during all his early years in the
anti-Catholic camp.

(4) Lastly, and covering the whole story, we must
seize the essential fact that the Netherlands had been

---

[2] He came to be called "William the Silent" after an uncorroborated story
which he told only in his own praise and which is manifestly a falsehood.
He pretended, later in life, that, as a young man, he had gone out riding
with the King of France, who had revealed to him a monstrous plot for
exterminating all the opponents of the Catholic religion, and how he, listen-
ing to this recital, had deceived his host, who believed him sympathetic, by
a brief ambiguous answer and silence.

formed by the mild, prosperous, and exceedingly popular Burgundian rule. They had been essentially a Burgundian Province. It was their Lords, the Dukes of Burgundy, and their paternal and well-received ordinances which had given a common form to the Low Countries; it was they who had increased the power and freedom of the little local town governments, who had deferred to and even deliberately fostered the free expression of opinion by the commercial and aristocratic bodies called the "Estates" of each province, and who had made the old civic customs of those great commercial towns, which were so proud of and attached to their traditions, take firm root.

Philip II, King of Spain, was the natural heir of these Burgundian founders, but he did not continue to rule the Netherlands in a Burgundian fashion; he tried to rule them in a Spanish fashion—and therein lay the whole tension between governor and governed. Things natural and right in Spain (a country living under the military conditions of a triumphant reconquest from Islam) were wholly unsuited to the Netherlands. For instance, absolute monarchy, taxes imposed from above without the consent of the taxed, as they are in all modern countries to-day, etc., were normal to Spain. They were not normal to the Burgundian Netherlands. They were quite alien. With that went the use of Spanish soldiery, the presence of Spanish Government, the suppression of ancient local endowments, the filling of Church places with Span-

iards, the introduction of the Spanish judicial methods. All these things, especially the Inquisition, were
offensive and violently irritant to the people of the
Netherlands, poor as well as rich.

Such is the scene upon which the Drama of the
Netherlands revolt is about to be played. Its inception was mainly the fault of Philip II. Its disastrous
conclusion in splitting the Netherlands into two—a
model of the great disruption of Europe—a catastrophe from which Europe still bleeds, was mainly
the fault of the Calvinist spirit and its predominance
among the rebels during the later phases of the war.
Had the Netherlands continued to form one State,
Spain would have been compelled to grant local
autonomy but Religion would have been saved, and,
with the Netherlands remaining one State there
would have been no Great War in 1914. What prevented the Netherlands from remaining one State was
the cutting in of the Calvinist element in the midst
of what had been a united patriotic movement.

When Philip II acceded to the Kingdom of Spain
and so much else (the New World, the possessions in
Italy, the relics of Burgundy, the Netherlands, etc.),
he committed the capital error of imposing Spanish
conditions upon a country wholly different in tradition and spirit from his own. He put in Spanish garrisons, Spanish administrators, and even Spanish
Churchmen, as well as a Spanish method of administration.

It must be said in his favour that there would have

been a grave problem for any man in attempting to maintain the unity of his realm while preserving the very separate character of the Lowland provinces; but a solution should at least have been attempted, and he did not attempt it. This error in policy resulted in a universal protest throughout the Low Countries, which grew rapidly in the course of a few years.

The protest was against three main grievances. (1) An alien soldiery, which irritated the populace. (2) The administration of affairs in the main by new and alien men instead of in the old traditional fashion by provincial assemblies of local nobles, and councils of rich merchants in the towns. (3) The making of new ecclesiastical benefices arbitrarily and the giving of ecclesiastical places to Spaniards. To these may be added a fourth, of which much more was made later, but which was already of considerable importance, the dissatisfaction with the Spanish form of the Inquisition.

The mass of the Netherlands, like that of most districts in the West as early as 1560-70, was Catholic in tradition and temper; but the grave peril presented by Calvinism to the only religion and culture which they cherished would have been met by them in a very different fashion from the way in which Spain met it. The Spanish Inquisition was devised against Jews and Mohammedans by a State which had only lately triumphantly freed itself from Mohammedan pressure backed by Jewish guidance. There was no problem of the kind in the Netherlands, and to apply the methods of the Spanish Inquisition to the Netherlands was to mistake the local conditions altogether.

But we must clearly understand that at the outset, and for many years to come, the problem was not essentially a religious one. It was economic and political: a demand for tolerable taxation after traditional models.

Thus the man who was so heroically to defend Haarlem against Spanish troops many years ahead was a Catholic. Again, the Catholic monks and prelates themselves were particularly exasperated, first, at being ousted by foreigners; secondly, at a later phase, by the unauthorised and dreadful pillage committed against the Church's wealth and priests by the mutinous and ill-paid Spanish troops.

The first protests, then, were universal. They were not exactly national, for the Netherlands were not a nation: but they were full of the very strongest local spirit; the spirit of those great rich towns which were then, and are again to-day, the commercial fruit of the Rhine Valley, and the exchanges of Northern Europe.

It was the nobles who took the lead in the protest, and among them the wealthiest and most important house, that of Orange, of which the present heads were native to the province of Holland.[3]

---

[3] The word "Holland" in the story of the Netherland revolt does not mean what we mean to-day in England by the word, the whole country of seven provinces; but only one of those provinces, the "Hollow Land" within the Dykes, to the north; the land of Amsterdam and Haarlem.

The nobles, here as everywhere, had their own axe to grind. They were not pure-souled patriots; on the contrary, they were more cosmopolitan than any other class. They acted in the main from two motives combined; first, anger at their loss in revenue and power after the introduction of Spanish officials; secondly (what moved their class throughout Europe during the religious wars), the opportunity of becoming immensely richer and more powerful through the destruction of monarchy.

Things came to a head when three young nobles, of whom Orange's brother was one, met at Spa in the autumn of 1565, and agreed to promote an active protest which might be called, by those whom it opposed, a revolt. When the fighting season of the next year, 1566, opened, the movement had gained great masses of the populace, and was very violent. And in the movement this is to be particularly noticed, for, in the first place, it explains what follows, and, in the second place, it is invariably softened down or given wrong values in the anti-Catholic textbooks of our schools and universities, and notably in such an unscrupulous partisan as Motley.

There was a wild, savage outburst, composed of every element destructive to society. Whenever a revolt is launched there is danger of that; but the elements of disorder were so numerous in the case of the Netherlands in 1566 that the danger was peculiarly grave. The small minority of Calvinist enthusiasts may be called the heart of the anarchy; but they were joined, of course, by every man who had a grievance; and it was a moment when most men had a grievance. Their worst action was the abominable torture of monks. But what struck onlookers more was the wanton destruction on an enormous scale of every sort of work of art, especially in religious buildings. You may go into Antwerp to-day, for example, and marvel why it is so bare. It is the work of 1566. It looked for a moment as though society would fall to pieces in the raging storm.

It must be remembered that it was in this atmosphere that the nobles, whom some one or other had called (we know not who nor when) by the nickname of "The Beggars," [4] took the opportunity of direct action against the legitimate but most unwise Government. That Government had not on the spot forces adequate to deal with the situation, and when the nobles (and the burgesses who followed them) presented demands (which were an ultimatum) at Brussels in that same year, 1566, and presented them in public force, almost in military array, there was nothing for the King of Spain to do but to fight, or to admit the dissolution of his realm.

He fought; and he did what any other ruler of the day would have done; he sent the best general he had, the Duke of Alva, with what he hoped was a sufficient force—seventeen thousand men.

When that force appeared in the Netherlands everything bowed down before it. Orange, as might

[4] The French word "*Les Gueux*."

have been expected, fled the country. Alva proceeded to a thorough investigation of the recent anarchy, and to executions upon a large scale. He had a complete success within eighteen months, indeed, within a year; and had he stopped there the trouble in the Netherlands might have been at an end. Even those who provoke anarchy do not like its consequences, and people in the Netherlands had had such a taste of anarchy that they did not want it to begin again, and were glad enough at its repression—though that repression was severe and though it came at the hands of the foreigner.

It was at this moment, however, that the second and much graver mistake was made. The Spanish Government, through the agency of Alva, imposed a new and (to the Netherlands) monstrous form of tax.

It must be noted that throughout all these struggles the Spanish King was handicapped by lack of resources, coupled with the immense extent of his dominions. Wherever you have widespread dominions, you find that: the tendency to disperse power, or rather the inevitability of such dispersion. He would never have enough men or money to impose a gravely unpopular measure upon any one province. And as for sea-power, he was far weaker in *that* than the teeming Netherlands ports.

Next we must remember that the wealthy inland towns were the best sources of revenue he had in all Philip's enormous possessions. It was this that tempted him.

The new tax (which was imposed by levy, but, after all, voted by the Estates) was proposed in March, 1569. It was of triple character: (1) a one per cent capital levy, not to be renewed; (2) a five per cent tax, as, we might say, stamp duty, on sales of land—these were the first two items, and neither of them was onerous. But the third was disastrous. It was proposed to levy (3) *a ten per cent tax on all trade transactions.* That, of course, was impossible and ruinous. It was upon a Spanish model, and in agricultural Spain it would have applied. In a mercantile community it was manifestly disastrous and unwelcome. How could people who lived by buying and selling goods over and over again pay a ten per cent tax on every transaction?

This it was which really provoked the final revolt and led to the ruin of Spanish power in the northern part of the Low Countries. There was a boycott, resistance, the shutting up of shops, the refusal to trade, and a false policy of attempted repression. What might have happened no one can say. Alva might have yielded in the long run, or, alternatively, the erroneous form of taxation might have failed, as bad taxes sometimes do, by exhausting the very source of revenue it was trying to tap. Spain might yet have retraced her steps or have compromised when, in April, 1572, came the stroke which changed the whole situation.

How the Reformation Happened

If you will look at a map of Belgium and Holland to-day, including a strip of northern France, including Arras, Lille, Dunkirk, and the belt along the Belgian frontier, you have the Netherlands as they were in the spring of 1572. They were seventeen provinces. Calvinism was then scattered all over the place (as a minority), perhaps somewhat stronger in the north, but not very much so. The bulk was still strongly Catholic.

You will note on such a map what the possession of the mouth of the Meuse and the main mouth of the Rhine, and the mouth of the Scheldt, would mean in any campaign. These rivers and their canals are the arteries of all the plain and its communications. The great inland towns all depend upon them, either as ports or standing on their banks.

Now the mouths of all these rivers come out together on one small stretch of coast next the province of Zeeland. Those who held that key could prevent munitions and soldiers and money coming in by sea, and could put a Government with a base so very distant as that of the Spanish Government to extreme difficulties. You will further note on such a map that there is a mass of maritime and river ports connected by canals with the whole system of the Rhine, Meuse and Scheldt. There are Antwerp, Rotterdam, Amsterdam, and so on. Nine-tenths of the great commercial cities communicated by water. And a good half of them were within a few hours' sail of the sea.

The Universal Battle: 1559-1572

From the northern ports sundry seamen, who called themselves "The Beggars of the Sea," in imitation of the original leaders (now crushed) by land, had begun a sort of piracy, first against Spanish commerce and transports, then against pretty well any one. Their very presence is an example of how difficult or impossible it was for Spain to fight successfully in these distant northern waters with all the other things she had to do upon every known sea-way of the world. In the spring of 1572 these irregular rovers heard that the little port of Brielle was ungarrisoned, and seized it. And immediately afterwards they so seized Flushing. They held henceforward the mouths of the rivers.

It was a capital event. They were never dislodged. Orange returned, and declared himself Calvinist in 1573. The two provinces of Zeeland and Holland became the scenes of a new resistance.

It is very important to note this seizure of the mouths of the rivers, and the way in which water dominated the issue. It was the water defences which enabled the provinces below sea-level, with their power of flooding, to keep up the struggle. It was this which concentrated Calvinism in the north (for into Zeeland and Holland returned a host of immigrants who had fled from Alva), and thenceforward the final success of Alva was impossible. Spanish ships, or rather ships in the Spanish interest, were destroyed upon the Zuyder Zee. Though many sieges laid by the Spaniards were successful, that of Alkmaar failed. And what was further of overwhelming importance was the fact that the small Spanish forces fell into arrears of pay. Alva resigned.

Henceforward the Battle in the Netherlands had reached its turning-point, as it had elsewhere at the same moment. With 1572 we begin to see the future shaping. France will keep tradition. Revolt in its favour in England has failed. In Scotland the new forces of European disruption are confirmed. As for the Netherlands all that wealthy territory has fallen apart. The North has seceded. The South stands firm. The results still endure.

CHAPTER VI

The Defence

BY 1572 Moral Anarchy in Europe has lasted over fifty years. The old Unity is hardly remembered. During all that lifetime the disruption of Christendom has increased, during the last third of the century active civil war had broken out between the hostile groups into which Europe had become torn. Yet all the while authority seemed incapable of asserting itself; that age-long Christian culture which had made us seemed paralysed, incapable of its own defence. The confusion had had time to become habitual to all men's minds, the mood of conflict to have become permanent, and thus the final falling apart of our civilisation to have become inevitable.

Why such delay? In the difficult problem of the Reformation an answer to that question is imperative, for the tardiness of the reaction is perhaps the main cause of our still increasing chaos.

To appreciate *how* tardy was the reaction consider the dates:

Luther makes his first protest, followed by tumultuous German enthusiasm, in 1517. Till 1559, for *forty-two years*—all the useful part of a human life

[209]

—Europe is in turmoil. Nothing seems to be decided, no definite issue seems to be taken.

Young men entering public life in any form at the moment when the quarrel began in 1517 were over fifty in 1549. By 1559, when the armed struggle began, they were already old men. Why was not a Council immediately summoned to deal with the mighty peril? Why did not the Church Universal act?

There are three considerations which between them answer the question. They are worthy of close attention because upon the delay to re-establish unity, authority, discipline, turned all that was to come.

1. The first consideration is this: The official organisation of the Catholic Church had been thrown suddenly into disarray. It had been caught, as they used to say of sailing ships, by a squall "all standing." It had no immediate case. There had been gross and universal corruption, there had further been for so long a growing scepticism and indifference that the power of the clerical organisation to reform itself was numbed and atrophied. Attack from without was therefore easy, rapid, and explosive; reform from within was apparently impossible; the complicated machinery was ill-kept and incapable of rapid re-adjustment. Under so violent a strain the gear jammed. And the Papacy, which controlled all, was in the worst case of all.

When any threatened institution is to blame and knows itself to blame, what soldiers call the "initia-

The Defence

tive" passes to its enemies. It is so, for instance, to-day with what is called Industrial Capitalism. Industrial capitalism is based upon two things which all sane men admit, the right to property and the advantage, economic and political, of individual freedom. Yet, through abuses of them, both property and freedom are to-day sick and their defence rings hollow.

Obviously the perfect thing to do in such cases,—if there were no conditions of matter, time and space, if most men were intelligent, pure in motive, and heroic, instead of being, as most men are, stupid, corrupt and cowardly—would be to perform what the Catholic Church herself calls Penance. Obviously the attack upon the Catholic Church would have had no success if all the officials thereof in the early sixteenth century had themselves come forward in a body denouncing their own guilt; the pluralities, the lay appropriations, the shame of their worldly lives, the gross scandals of impurity, the oppression of the poor, the exaggeration of mechanical aids to religion, the occasional use of fraud in it, the widespread use of extortion in clerical dues and rents, the chicanery of clerical courts. If the very many church officials who were guilty of evil living had beaten their breasts, repented and turned anchorite; if the very many who were swollen with riches had abandoned them and given them to the poor, if such of the cultured renaissance prelates as had come to ridicule the Mysteries had suddenly felt the wrath of God—then all would have righted. So fruitful is repentance.

How the Reformation Happened

But men do not act thus after long habit. It is only after they have felt the consequence of wrong-doing, and often not then, that they admit reality. Repentance, which should precede chastisement, is commonly its consequence.

2. The second consideration proceeds from, and is connected with, this first: the temper of the troops was all to the advantage of the attack. The attack was intense, fanatical, therefore unscrupulous. Let no one be shocked by this last word, for it is truthful. Fanatics *are* unscrupulous precisely because they are sincere upon a narrow issue. The attack upon the power of the priesthood, therefore upon the organisation of the Church, therefore upon the very nature of the sacramental system, therefore upon doctrine, therefore upon the unity of Christian life, therefore upon the whole culture of Europe (for such was the logical order of events) believed in itself profoundly. Its hatreds were of the flaming sort.

In such an attack you have crudity, but you have energy. Now, as I have said, it always takes some time for the old-established thing on its defence to wake up. An answer to attack upon tradition can always be found, but the traditional thing, being general, popular, and having become based upon routine turned to a kind of instinct, having long lost the habit of analysis, takes some time in finding it again. It is so with any social habit attacked to-day —Patriotism, on family life or property. It defends itself blindly, all the first clear arguments are with the enemy.

3. The third consideration is equally attached to the first two; it was the very fact that the body of church officials was weakened which gave opportunity to its enemies. A sick state is attacked by its enemies, a strong man is not; a man in authority, weakening, is attacked by his dependents; a powerful man in authority is not. In other words, the official organisation of the Church badly diseased in the old age of the medieval world, had to recover its health before it could successfully meet an offensive which had developed very far before resistance could begin.

The whole body of Church officialdom was weakened, and by this I do not only mean weakened from within by corruption or worldliness in its Hierarchy, I also mean weakened from without by the political development of Europe since the Black Death, that is, during the century and a half before the Reformation. The Papal Schism and the growth of Nationalities had obscured that universality which is of the very essence of the Catholic Church.

Such would seem to be the main causes of that fatal halt. But in spite of all these elements of delay, the *attempt* to call the necessary council came early.

The first idea that occurred to the Papacy when the storm grew loud was to summon such a Council, and it is worth remarking (though the matter is but a coincidence) that Charles V, then Emperor (it was during the few years of the original turmoil after Luther's protest), suggested Trent as the proper town for meeting. Trent was on the main road from the Germanies into Italy, and it was at Trent, as we all know, that the final Conference took place.

Why was it that for years and years the idea remained inoperative? Why was it that the signatures finally attached to the conclusions of the Council of Trent are not so attached until 1563, *nearly forty years* after the great Emperor had first made that proposal? Why is it not till full forty years later still that you get the final Bull *Benedictus Deus* sealed by Pius IV?

The anti-Catholic thesis still dominating most of our textbooks will have it that the fault lay with the Papacy. It was, they tell us, the successive Popes between Leo X and Paul III (1517-1534) who, during those deplorable seventeen years balked Christendom of the great general assembly which would have healed it. They might talk of, they did not at heart desire, a General Council. Their secret opposition was due to this: that for more than a century past General Councils had been the antagonists of the Papal power, makers and unmakers of Popes. The Papal Schism had made such Councils too powerful and had even raised in them the novel claim that they, not Peter, ruled the Church. A revival of such Councils the Popes feared and therefore it was (we are told) that the Popes obstructed the meeting of yet another Council to deal with the urgent needs of the time.

It is a myth and false. Like all myths it has its elements of truth. It is true that the policy of calling a general Council was perilous. It is true that there were occasions when the Popes thought the moment inopportune, but it was not Papal action which in the main so fatally postponed the Assembly.

What perpetually delayed this necessary Synod of all Christendom, even after it had been convened, was the power of the lay Princes exercised at the expense of the Papacy. What made it impossible for so long to call a Council at all was the fact that the Universal Church no longer governed itself. The independence of the Church which all the early Hierarchy had steadfastly proclaimed, which the first Christian Emperors of Rome had confirmed, which centuries later, St. Gregory VII (often in England and Germany called Hildebrand) re-established, which Innocent III raised to its fullest power, and which was the glory and security of the great thirteenth century—was gone. Each province had become national under its Prince. The Kings of England, of France, could restrain their local prelates from participating.

Let it be noted that the freedom of the Catholic Church has revived since the French Revolution in a way which men little expected. To-day, should the Pope summon a General Council, every member of the Hierarchy throughout the world would respond to the summons. Nothing but physical disability, or some strong local necessity for absence would prevent the presence of each individual at that Council. Yet the attempt to summon a General Council for the healing of Christendom in this mortal crisis of the sixteenth century failed for half a lifetime. Even when it finally succeeded (as in truth it did), how shrivelled it seems in size and how maimed in numerical force compared with the majestic gatherings of the early Church, or, for that matter, of our own day!

We have but to follow a sequence of dates to see how this perpetual postponement of the Council was a civil and political crime proceeding from the lay power.

While the Mohammedan was thundering at the gate and while the various Princes in Germany were weakening the Empire, the Pope's envoy was proclaiming that "next summer" (that is, in 1530, after more than *twelve years* of raging spiritual anarchy), the Council would be gathered at Augsburg; but the very men who had at first most clamoured for it, the rebellious German Princes, refused it.

The next year again, 1531, it was actually agreed on. But Francis I prevented it, acting thus as a political move against his enemy, the Emperor.

Next year again, 1532, Henry VIII of England (then in the height of his confused personal quarrel with the reigning Pope) vetoed the request of that

Pope to let the Prelates of England join such a Council.

For fifteen further years, from 1534 to 1549, that man who was determined on the achievement of the thing in spite of such intolerable interference, Paul III, insists and nearly carries it through, against the political opposition of the lay governments. The summonses are issued for the Council to meet at Mantua, and the first session is called for the spring of 1537. It was not too late, perhaps, for such a "Council of Mantua" to have put things right. Not twenty years of disturbance had passed. Men still remembered the better times and desired their return. But no such Council met. Again both the spiritual and the secular troubles arise; the protesting Princes of Germany will not commit themselves to an admission that they are part of the universal body of Europe, they refuse their subjects' presence. The King of France, still playing with the idea of complete independence from that same Body of Europe (the national idea), does not exactly refuse, but makes impossible conditions. Even the Duke of Mantua objects to the Council meeting in his territories. The Pope insists. If Mantua will not do, let them come to Vicenza in the next year, 1538. The aristocracy of Venice objects to Vicenza. In 1542 (it is already eighteen years since the first proposal) the matter appears to be settled by a refusal on the part of authority to haggle further; a Council is imperatively ordered by the Pope—but again France opposes, and a wretched meeting of "some few" turn up: only to be dispersed again. The Council has not begun.

At last, as one might say in despair, there appears some sample—it is little more—of that universal gathering which all common sense as well as Christian faith demanded. The thing does happen.

A Council met at Trent in 1545, and it was in the early January of 1546 that a Mass of the Holy Ghost opened its deliberations. But how many of the Hierarchy were present, in the face of lay opposition?—twenty-four! Four Archbishops and twenty Bishops.

I am not writing even the most general outline of this effort maintained by the Pope against such difficulties. It is enough to remark that the Council, thus hampered and belittled, did a work not only prodigious in extent, but final. The work was done by great theologians, experts in the law of the Church, and, in the consideration of sacred things, by the Generals of the Great Orders, by the chief Churchmen of the time, and notably through the guidance of that great man, St. Charles Borromeo. It defined in everything. It established a rigid discipline. It saved the Catholic Church on the edge of dissolution. On this account, because it defined, ordered and imposed so much, do the enemies of the Church continue to abuse it. They accuse it of making Catholicism a new, a narrow, a mechanical thing, with its precision of rule and strengthening of central authority. But their motive is apparent. They are vexed that the Church, by such an action, was saved.

Even as the Council sat the refusals of lay help continued, though the membership somewhat grew. Elizabeth was asked to send representatives and refused, just as Francis I and Henry II of France had begun by refusing to send representatives in order to play their political game against the Empire. When, therefore, the work was concluded, in the December of 1563, those of the Hierarchy who subscribed out of all Christendom were not two hundred; to be accurate, one hundred and ninety-two.

I think you have in the story of the Council of Trent (which I advise any one interested in that chief event of our race, the Reformation, to read with care) as good an example as you could find of what difficulties we were fighting and of why the Catholic Church was so barely saved.

The Council of Trent was the official action which, so fatally delayed, preserved what could be preserved: not the Unity of Europe, indeed, but the life of the Catholic Church.

Side by side with this central and universal action began to arise subsidiary elements of defence, soon turning into a counter-offensive. A reformation of the Clergy proceeded apart—notably in Rome itself, and after the Council, under the influence of St. Philip Neri. The Press was at work; a new Catholic Apologetic acquired vigour and momentum. But the main factor in the resistance and the recovery of Catholicism, in what may be called "the counter-offensive," was the rise of that body known to-day as the Jesuits.

The Clerks Regular of the Society of Jesus (for that is the full term), or, shortly, the "Society of Jesus," was the product of one of the most remarkable men in the history of our race, the worthy creator of his achievement, St. Ignatius of Loyola. He was the son of a Basque landed family. His great religious experience, falling in his thirtieth year, was coincident with the first years of the troubles. It came in 1521, within a few months of Luther's burning the Pope's Bulletin. Yet it is not till thirteen years later that even the smallest true organism appears, in 1534; not till five years after that that the constitution of the new body is sketched out; not till 1540 that it is confirmed by a Papal Bull, and even then on a small scale only; not till 1543 that it is permitted expansion.

It is, then, hardly an active force beginning its great mission before the end of what I have called the Period of Debate. All the first thirty years of increasing confusion in morals and doctrine had been at work before this instrument of order is beginning its career.

The first question we have to answer is, again: Why such a long delay?

We shall answer that question better if we put another one: "By what miracle did such an instrument appear at all?" No one had dreamed of it; its young founder had at first no plan of it. The idea grew for many years. The final acts which brought it into full being did not come in a process deliberately willed by human agents; but, as it were, from unseen power working towards an unexpected end. Lastly, it did not turn to the great work which it effected until it had already come into existence for a purpose somewhat different. I think it true to say that had there been a thing mechanically planned from the beginning to do what the Jesuits finally achieved, such a plan would have failed. I think it true to say that the dominating part they have played to the advantage of Europe was only possible in a thing thus developed, incidentally, from step to step and therefore so tardy in appearance.

That St. Ignatius was a gentleman, a Basque, and a soldier are three qualities inferior to his quality of sanctity; but they are all significant. The thing he made had breeding, it had the Basque iron in it, and —above all—it was essentially military; its military quality gave it—under God—the success which it obtained. Yet see with what considerable deliberation, like a natural growth, that thing arises.

First came St. Ignatius' own conversion, following on a wound received at the siege of Pampeluna. Then for years a purely private interior experience, full of all that trial which the saints in such years endure. A very small company of friends gathered round. But while the spiritual cause fell, as I have

said, in 1521, it is only at the Assumption in 1534
that this little band of seven men (of whom only one
was a priest) went from the University of Paris over
to Montmartre and there banded themselves together
in a simple fellowship. In 1539 the idea thus seeded
was complete, and had taken for all essential purposes its external form, and the "Institute" drawn up
by St. Ignatius was submitted to the Holy See.

There was in its idea something so novel that we
can well understand why it lay at the point of rejection by authority. It was the conception of a religious society rather than an Order, wherein the
office should not be said in choir—this for the purpose
of greater mobility; where obedience should be absolute, with none of those corporate qualities in government (democratic, as we now loosely term them)
which attached to all the older Orders.

This absolute obedience was to be essentially military in quality, therefore strictly monarchic and hier-
archic. The units of the fighting force existed for the
purposes of the whole body, and those who are ready
to criticise a discipline of this kind seem to forget that
it has been the necessary essential of every efficient
fighting force since man took up arms. Being Catholic, one exception only lay to this conception of an
entire discipline, to wit, the right of refusal in what
was sin. A soldier has not even that by the rules of
an army, though his moral right remain. In this
new ecclesiastical force that exception was formally
admitted. For the rest the military idea coloured all.

Yet was the objective of that army not defined when the army was made. It was at first in the mind of St. Ignatius and his followers to take up the age-long war against Islam. Only later were they thrown upon the new and (as it grew to be) more pressing front of spiritual rebellion in Europe.

They were missioners, too, of course, and from their origin the world was full of their effort among the heathen. But their main part in the story of our race, and especially in that of the Reformation, is their recovery of what seemed, humanly speaking, a losing cause: I mean the Cause of the Faith in the sixteenth century.

The founder died in 1556. It was two years later, just at that critical date to which attention has been called so often, 1558-1559, the opening of the period of conflict, that final constitutions were adopted. From that moment onward the struggle was incessant. Before the first lifetime is ended the new combatants have largely decided the issue in France, have helped to save what was saved in the Netherlands, have recovered great areas in the Germanies, may be said to have snatched from its peril the hesitating society of Poland.

Those who speak of the failure of the Jesuits in what they attempted and still attempt do not understand the nature whether of success or of the Faith. They do not see that a thing designed for forlorn hopes, for the most difficult of situations, an instrument especially thrown against the positions of greatest peril and least opportunity, is to be measured not by what is unattainable, but by what is attained. For instance, it was the Jesuits who attempted with peculiar heroism that effort in England which the able, despotic and highly organised Government of Cecil, grown more practised with every day and reposing with every day upon a larger body of lapsed Catholics, had made almost inevitably successful. The Jesuits, for all the tortures they suffered and for all their hardly human constancy, did not save England as they saved Poland. But who else made anything like that effort against such odds?

This sweeping success throughout our civilisation (for such it was) which attended the new fighting force of the Catholic Church had stiffening it, as armies have, a certain *morale*. It insisted upon two things essential to the moment and to the combat: personal rectitude, and learning. It turned the scale of discussion, putting all the best weapons into Catholic hands, so that to the very Jesuit philosophers, and notably to the great Suarez, were opponents themselves compelled to turn for argument. Further, they thought out and made of one piece, solid and permanent, a whole new system of education which became the model for Europe, which remains to-day the basis of all the best instruction in the traditional schools of the Continent.

Such was the chief instrument of the counter-offensive. Such are the reasons for its tardy appearance; but such also is the picture of its achievement.

The Defence

It did not prevent the catastrophe. Who could, so late? But it recovered all that could be recovered, and on account of its strength and its power to realise its ideals of victory has it been the chief target of those who, from whichever quarter, desire the obliteration of the Catholic name.

It is rather an irony—history is all ironies—that the name associated with such grandeur originated as a nickname. It came from the century before the Reformation, a disparaging term for one who has the Holy Name perpetually on his lips in ordinary speech and in canting fashion. It was taken up by Calvin against the Society as a term of abuse—for that great man clearly scented out where the strength of his enemies lay. It has passed into current speech in a number of twisted forms, and it is no small tribute to the high intelligence which the name "Jesuit" connotes that it is particularly associated with the complete analysis of moral problems. Your plain blunt man who spends his days in swindling his fellows and satisfying such poor appetites as he may possess, will call "Jesuitry" whatever demands an exact attention to a difficult point in morals. Such a man after lying freely and in good set terms upon the value of his wares, deceiving vendor and purchaser, protesting his integrity, will be shocked at the definitions of Escobar (which at the best he may hear at fourth hand) upon special cases of mental reservation.

The Society grew in strength as the division of Christendom proceeded. It evangelised the furthest

Asia. It formed in youth the governing classes of what it had preserved for the Catholic culture. It directed the recovery of Europe. It was the adviser of Governments. Its power bred friction between itself and the very Authority which it had arisen to defend—to save. It was suppressed by that Authority. It was revived. It is with us and will remain.

If to-day a man may hear Mass in Warsaw or hope that the classics shall survive our modern decay, he owes it to the Society of Jesus.

CHAPTER VII

The Draw: 1572-1600-1648

THE "Universal Battle" of 1559-1572 had reached in the latter year a point where it was clear that neither side would obtain a decision. In England the Catholic rising had been crushed, but in France the Protestant nobles could never be master after the St. Bartholomew. In the Netherlands Alva's effort at recovering the whole had failed; the most was retained for Catholicism but the seven Northern Provinces had held out and checked him.

There was to follow a lingering struggle everywhere which, after thirty years or so at the turn of the century, was to end in a draw. The great conflict flickered out. It did not come to an end throughout the West of Europe at the same time. It was brought to a halt in France; then achieved in England; last in the Netherlands: but, before or after, everywhere in the West within a few years of 1600. In Germany a violent, belated rally followed the years 1618-1648. But that too failed, and the Germans remained divided.

France

In France, the battlefield, the conflict reached a preliminary settlement on the publication of the

Edict of Nantes, April 13, 1598. The great civil war on Religion had by then produced its effect.

That effect was the destruction of moral unity among the French people.

This is the point to be emphasised. The great French civil war, beginning as a war of religion and continued in the main as a war of religion, could not indeed—after the St. Bartholomew—make the Protestant gentry the masters of France. The popular fury had stopped that. But neither could the Catholic mass of the French people conquer the armed Protestant gentry. The end—the Edict of Nantes—was a compromise, by which a wealthy Protestant body remained entrenched within a Catholic nation, and was granted not so much toleration as peculiar and exceptional privileges: walled towns and fortresses of their own, law courts of their own, a special government peculiar to themselves. That situation was gradually modified, but its essentials endured for close upon a century. On this account France was, from that time onwards, divided. She has remained divided. For though Protestant doctrine dwindled, and first Deism and then a materialist Scepticism took its place, yet a united and strong Catholic culture, corresponding to the united and strong anti-Catholic culture of Britain, did not arise; and that is why France, in spite of the restoration of a strong monarchy and a nominal unity of religion, at the end of Louis XIV's reign, has never been able to take the permanent lead of Catholic culture in Europe; and that is why, as a

further consequence, Catholic culture has everywhere
been permanently weakened.

From the day of the St. Bartholomew, the violent
popular upheaval against the Protestant nobles, to the
promulgation of the Edict of Nantes is twenty-three
and a half years. But this long period was not one
ceaseless combat under arms. It was one of intermit-
tent wars.

The young King Charles IX died the second year
after, in May, 1574, and his still younger brother
(who had been elected King of Poland) succeeded
him at the age of twenty-three under the title of
Henry III.

This man, Henry III of France, was a curiously
mixed character. Young as he was, he had a great
reputation as a soldier; he had won two great victories
in the earlier civil wars. He was highly cultivated
and of a tenacious scholarship. He was not without
will power, and he had passionate fits of devotion.
But he was thoroughly diseased, in both body and soul.

The mark of the moment—1574—when Henry III
came to the throne, was a change in the character of
the civil war. Those who were discontented among
the Catholics, especially in the south of France,
joined with the main body of the old Protestant rebellion. The incapacity of the boy-kings, the unpopular government of the Queen Mother, Catherine de'
Medici, a certain division between the north and the
south, more than anything the necessity for raising

revenue out of taxpayers ruined by ceaseless conflicts, led to this strange combination; and at the end of two years, in the spring of 1576, the armed resistance of the new alliance to the Crown led to a paper compromise called the Edict of Loches. The Protestant party (which meant the powerful revolted nobles) were given towns in which they could exercise their novel rites; there was a general indemnity; the Protestants were to share jurisdiction in half the superior courts of the country.

I have called it a paper compromise, because such an admission of division in the body politic produced violent protest from the mass of the people, especially in Paris, and there was formed, against allowing a compromise, the first League.

That word "League," meaning a strong association of Catholic France for the maintenance of religious and national unity, was to have a prodigious fortune.

The young King and his mother were concerned for one thing above all: the maintenance of the power of the Crown. They were not greatly concerned for religion, though the king as an individual was strongly Catholic. They were more concerned for the inherited authority of the monarchy. On the one hand, the son of the murdered Guise (the man who, to revenge his father's death, had let loose the populace in the St. Bartholomew) rivalled the power of the Crown by his popularity as Catholic leader of the nation. On the other, Young Henry of Bourbon, the King of Navarre, at the head of the Protestant nobles, was likely to become the heir to the throne. People already doubted whether Henry III would ever have a child. His one surviving brother seemed in a like case.

In 1585, things came to a head. The younger brother of the King, who had been the heir, was dead, and his distant cousin and brother-in-law, Henry of Navarre, was left remaining the sole legitimate heir. The French were passionately attached to their hereditary monarchy. They were at that time equally attached to their age-long national religion. But the heir to that monarchy was an opponent to that religion. It was a situation of intolerable strain.

The League, which had languished, or at any rate had not been able to affirm itself, acquired new power. Henry III, the monarch, and his mother, submitted sullenly to its dictation; but they watched their time to free themselves, for *their* main motive, I repeat, was the independence of the Crown from *any* control. Popular and Catholic or Aristocratic and Protestant: it irked them as much to be under a great Catholic noble (even though he were the leader of the mass of the nation, like Guise) as to be dependent on their cousin of Bourbon, who was heir to the throne. The League put forward Henry of Navarre's uncle, the Cardinal of Bourbon, a rather futile elderly gentleman, as their nominee for the Crown after Henry III.

With that you get the final phase of open war between the armed noble and Protestant faction and the unarmed, confused mass of the nation, the conscious and organised part of which was the populace of Paris.

Henry of Navarre called in German aid for himself and the Protestants. While the German forces were invading France to join him, he won his first victory, at Coutras in October, 1587; but immediately after, Guise, with his army, destroyed the German invaders. Things were therefore apparently in the balance when Paris, which had already declared itself with violence, began to turn against the King. For in spite of the King's submission to the League it was felt that this submission was half-hearted. The people of Paris were particularly inflamed by recitals of the persecution of the popular Catholic body in England. The League publicly exhibited in the streets large posters showing the tortures inflicted by a Protestant Government, and these showed graphically what a Catholic people might expect if it gave such a minority power. There were seen the strangling and disembowelling of living men, the racks and tortures in the inquisition chambers of Cecil. When Guise came back from the army to Paris in May, 1588, he was received with the violent popular enthusiasm of the whole city. Paris rose against the King, who fled.

The failure of the Spanish Armada rather more than two months later, at the end of July, the consequent weakening of Spain (which was, of course, backing the League and the French popular effort), impelled the King to summon a national parliament in his support. But the Huguenots abstained from the elections; no national conciliation came of the session; Guise was more powerful than ever, and two days before Christmas the King, at Blois, caused Guise and his brothers to be treacherously murdered while they were attending the Court.

It was this which decided all. A few days later the Queen Mother was dead, Paris was in a raging ferment against the Crown, and against the heir apparent to the Crown. Henry III, the King, joined that heir apparent, his cousin Henry of Bourbon, although Henry of Bourbon was at the head of the Protestant faction. Between them they cut Paris off from succour. They were besieging the town, when a monk coming out of that furnace of Parisian emotion found his way to the King in the enemy's lines at St. Cloud, and murdered him on August 1, 1589.

Henry of Bourbon, already King of Navarre, still a Protestant, was now legitimate King of France. He besieged Paris, which stood the strain of famine with amazing tenacity rather than admit the claim of the legitimate heir, because that legitimate heir was still at the head of the Protestant nobles. The price which the legitimate heir paid for appeasement was the acceptation of Catholicism. Henry of Navarre was formally reconciled with the Church, and was crowned King of France under the title Henry IV.

But the Catholic mass of the people had not really

won against their opponents, the Protestant nobles. There issued in the spring of 1598 what is the term of the whole affair, and is known to history as the Edict of Nantes.

It set up a State within a State; the Protestant minority small but immensely rich, and forming as large a proportion of the armed fighting titled class as it did a small one of the whole nation, was to be given that highly privileged position which I mentioned above. The more powerful gentry were to carry on Calvinist ritual publicly in their castles, the lesser ones privately in their houses; Protestants were to be admitted into every post, and into all the public bodies; most important of all there were to be a number of fortified towns handed over to the Protestants, with Protestant governors and garrisons, and these were to be maintained at the expense of the Catholic monarch and nation.

Such was the end of that drawn battle. We feel throughout Europe to-day the effect of that failure to achieve unity in France.

England

The English movement after the crushing of the great Catholic rebellion steadily followed the Cecilian plan of stifling the Catholic Church throughout the realm. This slow strangulation was finally assured of success in a process of thirty-three years, the years 1572 to 1605.

Here also, then, the general European conflict reaches its term at much the same time as in France and the Netherlands. By 1570-1572 whichever was, in each country, the side destined to ultimate success is already in power. After the failure of the Armada (1588) it is fairly certain that the Protestant part of the English nation will predominate; after the Gunpowder Plot (1605) and the second Cecil's careful nursing of it, it is certain that England will not be Catholic again, though nearly one-half of the people (in mere numbers) were still attached at that date in varying degrees to the national tradition in religion. Roughly speaking, at the end of the sixteenth century the main struggle is over in the West everywhere and the event decided, though one field still remains indeterminate—that of the German States, nominally under the control of the Empire.

We begin with Cecil's original triumph, the destruction of Norfolk, and his own peerage as Lord Burghley, which confirms him by 1572.

Following upon the reign of terror which had begun with the Catholic rising of 1569-1570 and the excommunication of Elizabeth by the Pope, the next fifteen years are filled with the prosecution of Cecil's plan.

He could now, since the bloody crushing of the rebellion and since Elizabeth's excommunication, continue and make permanent that reign of terror for which the rebellion had given its original excuse. Cecil's Terror was established to root out Catholicism

—and it succeeded. The poorer mass of a people will hardly ever be sufficiently attached to an old religion to withstand their master's abandonment of it save when it stands for an oppressed nationality. Those who compare the success of the French populace in their violent uprising against the Huguenots with the failure of the corresponding English efforts to maintain the national religion forget two essential things: first, that in the French case the Crown was, on the whole, with the populace; secondly, that in the English case the gentry, the natural captains in any struggle of that time, had been bribed with the loot of the Church.

With every year that passed the success of that new body of great fortunes (of which Cecil was the head, the spokesman, and by far the ablest manager) grew stronger as a new generation grew up which had no experience of Catholic influence. I have already described the futility of talking of these things in numerical terms and of asking at any given date what number of Englishmen were Catholic and what Protestant as though the terms stood then for what they mean now, two sharply divided cultures. Most men in the England of Elizabeth were Catholic in tradition and idea, not one in many hundreds had the rarest chance of Mass or communion, penance, marriage or orders. A minority only—large, but still a minority—would risk much, let alone life, to restore the Faith, though with armed aid that minority would have rapidly become a large and increasing majority.

The Draw: 1572—1600—1648

Even as early as the beginning of all this, in 1572, it was thirteen years since the general presence of Mass in the land had disappeared. The young man just entering public life in 1572 could barely recall the Mass as a vague memory of his early childhood. Within ten years more there was a whole generation to whom the general practice of Catholicism was unknown, and with whom there only remained the traditional words and phrases of a Catholic society, much, of course, of its ethics and of its social tradition, but of practice none, save here and there, in very few spots, under peril of death, and in dreadful secrecy.

And here it is important to point out to non-Catholic readers the falsehood of the contention that Cecil's policy was a religious compromise, as our textbooks pretend it to be—usually calling it "Elizabethan," as though the unfortunate Elizabeth was responsible for the innovation! Those who speak thus know nothing of the Catholic Church. There is no "compromise" between a unique thing and others alien to it, of different essence, opposed to that unique thing. Lemonade is not a "compromise" between wine and water, nor blue glass a compromise between purple and clear stainless panes.

The new religion which Cecil and his clique substituted for the old was indeed not Calvinist, though Calvinism was the one ideal strength set up against the Catholic Church. Cecil and his lot would not allow England to fall into Calvinism. They feared Cal-

vinism, because Calvinism was such a living, powerful thing that it might have swept them away. For
the object of these people was not to *establish* some
creed, good or evil, to which they were attached, but
to *prevent* a return to the old traditional society, on
the destruction of which their vast fortunes were
founded.

As for Elizabeth, we have seen in a previous chapter
what her true position was: the royal power was
still believed in by herself, and largely by those who
none the less controlled her. But if we seek in her
personality or will what happened in England, we are
quite off the mark. *In all major things she had to
yield*. For the royal power was already stricken at
the root and that of the rich was supplanting it.

Meanwhile, those who really governed continued
their course. They helped the Huguenots in France;
they helped the rebels in the Netherlands—first,
secretly, and then openly; they connived at the growing piracy against Spanish trade—and took care that
it further enriched themselves, standing in with those
who practised it—and the Queen had no choice but
to follow suit. She had not the strength to stop it:
so she must connive at it, and so conniving she might
as well take her share.

The climax of all this came in the determination,
taken in 1585-1586, to put Mary Stuart to death.
She had been a prisoner since her youth, that is, from
the age of twenty-six: first, under the conditions of
an imprisonment veiled but effectual; then, since

1570, a prisoner indeed. She had now passed her fortieth year and her doom was upon her.

The main reason which decided Cecil and his companions to put this unfortunate woman to death was the health of Elizabeth. It had always been perilous. Latterly (in the later '80's of the sixteenth century) it had become occasionally alarming. Mary's wretched son James, crowned King of Scotland, was under the power of Cecil's agents and allies. He had been brought up to abandon his mother and the religion of his fathers. To the Crown of England (after his mother) he was heir. If Mary could be got out of the way, there would be no obstacle to a continuous anti-Catholic policy. There was still far too strong a feeling in England to permit of keeping the Catholic Queen in prison after the last Tudor was dead, and Elizabeth's death would have meant civil war. In such a war Cecil and his adherents would have seen their huge new fortunes at least imperilled and more probably destroyed. Therefore Mary must die by force, lest Elizabeth's death by nature should come first and endanger them all. The method by which the conspirators attained their end was as follows:

They used an *agent provocateur*, what is called in our modern slang a "nark"; that is, a secret police spy who pretends to be one of the discontented, who leads them on to plan some actionable deed and then betrays them to his employers.

They sent this fellow over to Paris to urge the more militant Catholic refugees to some action against

Elizabeth. Their agent was successful, and, in particular, a most indiscreet, gallant young fellow, called Babington, fell into the trap. Opportunity was offered to Mary to correspond with the plotters, under what she was assured was complete secrecy. In reality the letters to and from her passed through the hands of Walsingham, the head of the secret police, and Cecil's man. Babington's group designed the murder of Elizabeth, the rescue of Mary Stuart, and her proclamation.

But that was not sufficient for Cecil's purpose. As an individual Babington didn't count. England was full of men who would have been glad to kill Elizabeth. *The point was to get Mary Stuart implicated in such a design to murder.* Then she could be accused of high treason and put to death.

Her secretaries were seized, and under the threat of torture they said that she had so written a letter approving Elizabeth's assassination. Now, if she had, it must have passed through Walsingham's hands; indeed, the very words incriminating her, and said to be in the letter, were quoted on Walsingham's authority. Yet Walsingham never showed the original. Mary denied having written any such words, and demanded that her letter should be produced. It was never produced. All that Cecil's agents put forward was a supposed copy, of the authenticity of which they offered not the least proof, and it was on the strength of this alleged copy *with no proof that an original existed,* that Mary was beheaded. Though Elizabeth would have desired Mary's secret removal as a rival, she was bitterly opposed to the public and official murder of Mary, for such an outrage made her directly responsible before Europe. Elizabeth was caught. The poor woman fought hard against signing the warrant, and then fought harder to prevent its being put into action. But she had to yield. The New Millionaires were her masters.

The deed had as profound an effect on the Europe of that day as the Bolshevist murders have had upon our own. It gave the King of Spain an opportunity to interfere and stop the perpetual piracy against his subjects' trade, and Cecil's support of the rebels in the Netherlands. He therefore prepared a fleet of transports, large, but with insufficient convoy ("Armada" is Spanish for fleet). It was to sail to the Straits of Dover, there embark men from the Netherlands army and bring them over to England. Had the army in succour of the English Catholics landed, there would have followed a great national rising in defence of the Faith. The opposition to the Faith, though spreading by this time among a large minority of English people, was as yet intense in but a small section of that minority, and would not have been strong enough to prevent the release of the Catholic majority. Cecil's effort would have been ruined and the Faith, which was still by tradition the habit of thought in much the most of Englishmen, would have been restored in its splendour. As for what

Elizabeth's attitude would have been in such a case, we know enough of her character and of her action while the issue was still doubtful, to make pretty sure of that. She would have accepted the change and kept her throne. She had acquired by this time a fine disgust for Cecil's new official religion, though she had had to accept it as the price of her crown.

But Philip's expedition failed (neither he nor his called it "invincible"). His ships were worse handled than the ships sent out against them from English ports (under Lord Howard of Effingham—one of the anti-Catholic clique and a partner to the killing of Mary Stuart) and under Drake, a bitter hater of the Faith as well as an excellent sea captain and unscrupulous thief. The Spaniards failed for many reasons, all connected with their inadequate armament and finance for holding world-wide, scattered and ill-provided dominions. To that inadequacy was added a misunderstanding of their task in these northern waters. Their ships could not sail as close to the wind as ours. Their fire was insufficient. Their troops were not ready to embark, and, as a final blow, the wind veered northwest at the critical moment and threatened the Spanish vessels (already slipped down weather to escape fire ships) with a lee shore. The wind then rose to a gale and compelled them to run before it up the North Sea. As Cecil's Government put it, "God blew," and they were dispersed. Elizabeth had held her hand throughout, so as to have a policy ready in case the landing had been effected.

When all the risk was over—but not before—she held a review of troops at Tilbury and appeared as victor.

After this the process of decatholicising England went on much faster and more successfully. Cecil himself died in 1598, but his dynasty continued; his son, Robert Cecil, an ugly, humpbacked dwarf with an enormous head and all the ability of his father—or more—succeeded to power.

By that time it was forty years since the Mass had been known by English people. Only the old men and women remembered the active presence of the Catholic Faith. All men in middle life were without experience of its ritual or of teaching in its doctrines —the younger men had not known it at all.

Even so, after Elizabeth's miserable death in 1603, and James's accession, the second Cecil still feared the power of the Catholic tradition in England. About half the nation still sympathised with it, though most of them by this time but vaguely. Still, it might return. There was as yet a large and determined minority of men who actively boasted the Catholic name, and under favourable conditions hosts would rapidly rally to them.

What clinched the business for good was the Gunpowder Plot. It was ostensibly a Catholic plot to destroy King and Parliament—in the case of Fawkes the motive was almost certainly genuine; the others may have been used by the Government. Whether Cecil started the thing, as his father's agents had started the Babington plot, we shall perhaps never know. It is probable, but not certain. What we do know is that Cecil was fully acquainted with it all along,[1] nursed it carefully, at the right moment dramatically exposed it, published several contradictory official versions all of which are, in different degrees, false, and created throughout England a horror of the attempt and a new feeling against the Catholic Church as a whole, which finally turned the scale. All the dull, careless, central mass without strong views would henceforward connect the Catholic name with menace of this kind, and from that moment—1605— the active Catholic cause is that of a fraction of England declining for a lifetime onwards, till, by the end of Charles II's reign, eighty years on, it is, perhaps, no more than a seventh or an eighth of the nation.

Yet even under the English Government, even under the Common Kingship of all the British Isles after James I's accession, the incomplete "Draw" was evident. Catholicism was defeated in Britain and destined at last to be eliminated there. But in Ireland the effort failed. Protestant government was established. The Catholic religion survived.

Such was the course of anti-Catholic success in this country during the last lifetime of its progress, from 1559-1605. It had found England a country familiar with schism, troubled by a small but fierce Calvinist

[1] The first date assigned to the conception of the Plot is March, 1604. The first hint we have of the Government's watching and "nursing" it is April, 1604. The pretended "discovery" is November, 1605. So it was "nursed" in secret by Cecil for the full eighteen months.

body: an England indifferent in practice, but Catholic in all its main traditions and temper. The Queen, Elizabeth, humanist, sceptical, and inheriting very bad health, presided over a movement in which she was overridden and mastered by the new fortunes based on the loot of religion. These, whether in the hands of old families like the Howards or of men from the street like the Cromwells, were the key to the whole affair. To preserve that enormous booty the Faith must be destroyed. There was all manner of exception and cross-current, but such was the main line of development. Controlling it—though but one among many such—the spokesmen and brains of it—were the Cecils, father and son, sprung from a hostelry in Stamford; the man of their second generation, William, the first Lord Burghley, was first secretary to the Council, then all-powerful Minister; the man of the third, his son Robert, the first Lord Salisbury, concluded the task. This Cecil dynasty covered the whole process and ruled England for fifty years till it had achieved its end. They remained wealthy (it was their chief object); they destroyed the Faith in England. The result of their labour endures.

The Netherlands

We have seen how Alva had attempted—and failed —to reduce the northern part of the Netherlands. Seven provinces maintained their secession: ten rallied to the legitimate sovereign as the struggle became more and more religious, less and less economic. Unpopular though Spanish rule might be it was preferable to Calvinism and the power of the merchant oligarchy.

That separation was maintained, and the Netherlands emerged from the struggle divided, as all Europe was divided, with a North (to-day called Holland) controlled by Protestants, and a Catholic South, today called Belgium; the Protestant part retaining a large body of Catholics under persecution.

The thing was typical of the drawn conflict everywhere. Its steps were as follows:

Alva had resigned in the critical year 1572 which marks the failure of the first great battle throughout Europe to attain a decision: the year of the St. Bartholomew which prevented an urgent decision in France; the year of Cecil's finally established power in England.

There was appointed in Alva's place Requesens, in 1574. He died in 1576, after attempting a policy of pacification. Perhaps that policy had come too late; perhaps it was taken for a sign of weakness. At any rate, by the time he died, it was clear that the secessionist provinces, among the wealthiest, and now definitely under Calvinist government, and with a properly organised army (which they could pay), were in a position to maintain an indefinitely prolonged war.

This was all the more evident from the fact that the continued lack of pay to the Spanish soldiery led them to open mutiny everywhere. They made good their arrears by pillage, committed terrible atrocities, and arrayed against them the Catholic clergy whose endowments and even persons they did not spare; with the result that during this period of indetermination after Requesens' death and before the arrival of a new Governor all the Netherlands seemed for a moment to have come together again in what was called the Pacification of Ghent. The native Catholic authorities, at any rate the wealthier of them, united with the wealthy Calvinists of the north in a sort of truce which they called a peace, and both faced the now decaying Spanish power. The reason the Catholics acted thus was the necessity for an army to defend them against the Spanish soldiery, which had got out of hand.

Philip nominated his illegitimate half-brother, Don Juan, the victor of Lepanto, to the Netherlands. He died within two years (in 1578), and there was then appointed such a man as might, had he appeared at the beginning of these affairs, have saved the Netherlands for Spain and for Catholicism. It was too late, but even so what he did was very remarkable.

The new Governor was Parma, a man thirty-three years of age, naturally vigorous, with a wide vision, capable of delay, and, what is of chief importance, capable of grasping the complexity of a situation. He saw that although there was an apparent truce between the two religious factions, yet it was but apparent, and that their presence side by side for any length of time would be impossible. He used the Catholic feeling in favour of his King and he used it successfully.

William of Orange saw what was going on, and had attempted to meet it by influencing the Estate to pass a sort of Utopian scheme by which the Calvinists should tolerate the Catholics in their Government, though the Calvinists by this time regarded the Catholics both as traitors to the Netherlands and as the enemies of God; while the Catholics should tolerate the Calvinists, though the Catholics regarded the Calvinists as Western society to-day regards the Bolshevists—people who had already massacred and wrecked wholesale and would destroy all that is worth having if they had the power. Such a scheme, had it worked, would have increased his own power and wealth greatly by making him the chief man in all the Netherlands. But this absurd and hypocritical scheme of Orange's was not born alive. And Parma's policy, which was based upon reality, legitimate government, and popular support won against it hands down. He recovered control of the troops; he reduced city after city; he brought security, and the Netherlands began to recover.

But the Calvinist merchant oligarchy of the Northern Provinces held out. In July, 1581, Philip at The Hague was solemnly declared deposed from his kingship, and one effort after another was made to get foreign princes to accept his succession and to undertake the Regency, in theory of all the provinces, in practice of the small district that still remained subject to the rebels. After William of Orange had been assassinated, in 1584, Elizabeth refused; the brother of the King of France, called Anjou, accepted, but failed miserably, retired and died.

Parma continued his successes. In 1585 he captured Antwerp, and the efforts of Cecil to play a part in these foreign affairs with English soldiers and money failed ridiculously under the incompetence of Leicester, Elizabeth's favourite. It is conceivable that even at this late hour, Parma might have had a final success, but for the exaggerated policy of his master, the King of Spain; for Philip just at that moment found himself compelled to face French power and had—as we have just read—also undertaken the project of invading England for the liberation of the Catholic majority in that country.

Even regarded as part of a general project for restoring Catholicism in the North, this project of a fleet bearing an army to relieve the English Catholics was too great a dispersion of forces. Regarded from the point of view of a statesman who should have appreciated how essential the Netherlands were to the power of Spain, it was a disaster. Even had the Armada succeeded, it would have been a disaster to the Spanish power in the Netherlands. For it dispersed forces for a new war. But the Armada failed. Meanwhile, this ordering of Parma to face southward and the withdrawal of Spanish strength from the real seat of action, which was against the northern rebels, was finally fatal to the full Spanish claim.

What followed was of necessity the gradual enfranchisement of the northern Netherlands from Spanish power, so that the whole of Parma's fine effort resulted in no more than the saving of the south (what to-day we call Belgium and a strip of northern France). Already the ending of the French religious wars and the newly consolidated power of Henry IV in that country was creating a formidable and permanent pressure against the southern border of the Netherlands.

The young son of William of Orange showed himself an excellent soldier (which his father had certainly not been). He consolidated his power to the east and to the south, till it nearly reached what we call to-day the frontiers of Holland; and as things now stood this new power was definitely for Calvinism, and for the suppression as completely as might be within its dominions of all Catholic worship and tradition among the very large proportions of its population who detested Calvinism and clung to their religion. The most important point in the strength of that new State (for such it now had become), was that it now fixedly held the mouths of the rivers.

In 1596 the independence of the seven provinces, thus united in declaring their detachment from Spanish rule, was formally recognised by Elizabeth's Government in England (now directed by the second Cecil, the original Cecil's son) and by Henry IV, the new master in France. In 1598 Philip died, and though the last signatures which confirmed the position were not given till 1609, we may say that by 1600 the work had been accomplished. A new Protestant State, destined to a comparatively brief but very great career, had arisen. The rising Protestant body in England was confirmed in its power against the Catholic masses. The prestige of Spain had been wrecked and the incapacity of that power to hold by force all that it was legitimately entitled to by inheritance had been exposed.

The strategic model of the Reformation, the struggle in the Netherlands, was accomplished.

The German Valley and Its Failure

We have seen how, by the early seventeenth century, the settling down of Europe into a permanently divided, double civilisation composed of two mutually hostile bodies, had been effected: in other words, how the Reformation had succeeded in detaching great districts, principally in the North, from the general religious body of our civilisation, and thereby creating in that civilisation a wound and disruption from which it has never since recovered.

But, strangely enough, there was one very important and large area—the Empire, standing in the middle of Europe, mainly German speaking, consisting of a vast mass of smaller and larger principalities and independent cities, all nominally under the ruler of Austria, who was their common Emperor—in which the whole question was on the point of being revived in those very years, the opening years of the seventeenth century, which had seemed elsewhere to have brought matters to a conclusion.

I say "strangely enough" because Germany was the very country in which the first great revolt against unity had shown itself. For half a lifetime the Protestant movement was regarded throughout Europe as a German thing in origin and character. It was not until Calvin had had his full effect, the second half of the sixteenth century, that this origin was modified. But to this day most men think of Protestantism as something essentially German and the German culture as its champion.

It seems surprising, therefore, to learn that when the main battle was over in France, England, and the Netherlands, Italy, Spain, Poland, and Scandinavia, it should have been revived just in that part of the world where one would have thought that it had been earliest concluded. But so it was. The Germans re-opened the whole issue, and in a fierce struggle the confused details of which are generally reckoned to stretch from 1618 to 1648 (that is why the conflict is called the "Thirty Years' War"), the issue hung doubtful—at any rate during the fiercest part of the fighting—whether all the German-speaking world would not be ultimately recovered for the Faith.

In point of fact, as we shall see, this belated effort failed, and ended in compromise, that is, in the break-

down of unity. Just as in France a powerful and
wealthy Protestant body had been permanently
formed, just as in the Netherlands the struggle had
ended in a division of Protestant North against the
Catholic South, also permanent, just as, in these
Islands the Irish Realm maintained the popular religion against the dominant Protestantism of Britain,
so in the great area of the Germanies the thing ended
in division; and to this day, as everybody knows, we
have two separate civilisations among the Germans,
the Catholic and the Protestant, of which the latter
holds the keys of power.

Yet the failure to re-establish Catholic unity among
the Germans in this tremendous and tragic struggle
was not due to a superiority in arms or in tenacity of
the towns and districts already long separated from
Catholic unity. It was due to another factor, which
was of capital and enduring effect upon the fortunes
of Europe—the genius of the French statesman Richelieu: the Bismarck of his time.

How this came to be so I will now describe.

I can, of course, only do so on the very simplest
lines in such few pages as these. But the essential
thing, especially for an English-speaking reader, to
grasp is the fact that the German result was due
to the intervention of French nationalism opposed to
the interests of the Catholic Church.

The way in which this paradoxical state of affairs
came about, the saving of the German Protestant culture from re-absorption into Catholicism by the

action of a French Cardinal—in his own country the tenacious enemy of Protestantism—was as follows:

The Empire, as we have already seen, though full of majesty and with a very great name of authority, had no strength corresponding to its apparent position. Indeed, that was the very reason which had produced the early success of the Reformers. The independent cities and the local princes could defy the Emperor. He was powerful in his own private dominions, Austria, just as every German prince and every German town government was powerful in its own private dominions; but over the princes and towns who were nominally his subjects, but not under his direct rule, not in his own district, he had very little hold.

Now at this late hour, in 1618, when the German settlement seemed to have reached finality for a full generation, the Emperor of the day, Ferdinand II, determined to restore, if possible, the ancient political strength of his titular position, and to make himself the real monarch of all Germany, as well as of those districts not German-speaking (Slav and Hungarian) in which he was also a king. He was in a strong position to act thus, for he was, perhaps, more solidly established after his election to the Imperial throne than had been any of his predecessors for a century past.

Now the Emperor's family, the Hapsburgs, stood for Catholicism as did the Imperial title. What was still regarded as the most powerful branch of the Hapsburg family governed Spain, much of Italy, and the wealth of the New World, and had saved the greater part of the Netherlands for the Church. This other branch—the Austrian branch, as it was called —with their capital at Vienna, were in the same air and position. The Imperial title, though elective, remained in the Austrian branch reign after reign, and the Emperor was by tradition the Defender of Catholicism, the opposition to which was still regarded as a political rebellion no less than a religious one.

When, therefore, the Emperor set out on this belated attempt to consolidate his power and to make the Empire a true kingdom with a powerful monarch, himself, and everybody else subject to the Crown, it was very nearly equivalent to saying that he would establish Catholicism everywhere if he were victorious. Not that the two sides divided into exactly defined camps of Catholic and Protestant, but they tended more and more to do so, especially when the Emperor issued an order that Church lands stolen since the last great compromise—nearly seventy years before—should be restored.

It looked in the earlier part of the struggle as though the Emperor would achieve his end. He was able to hire by far the stronger armies, commanded by the better generals.

But in France there was taking place a rapid consolidation of all the national forces under the Crown.

A modern organised nation was being produced with a strong central government, and every one subject to it. The author of this great work was Cardinal Richelieu, who rapidly rose to be all-powerful under the Bourbon King whom he served, Louis XIII, the son of Henry IV of Navarre.

At home, in France, Richelieu fought hard and successfully to reduce the power of the Protestant section, because division in religion and the giving of special privileges to a powerful wealthy minority weakened the nation. But abroad it was exactly the other way. Richelieu's object there was to prevent the arising on the east of France of a new strong consolidated German Kingdom under the Emperor, whose power would threaten the French throne and people and all Richelieu's achievement within his own country. Richelieu, therefore, supported the Protestant cause in Germany against the Emperor, and when that cause was in danger of defeat he called in the best general of the day, Gustavus Adolphus, King of Sweden, who had also the best army of the day under his orders.

Gustavus Adolphus accepted French pay to the tune of a million livres, and fought in Germany as the champion of the Protestants. He had a sudden and startling success, and though he died in 1632, still comparatively young (in his thirty-eighth year), and though all was in a very complex situation (the Emperor of the moment could not depend upon his best general, and there were any number of cross-currents at work), yet it was the appearance of the King of Sweden in the field which checked Imperial victory.

Richelieu lived on till 1642, always, on the whole, supporting the Protestant cause in Germany, though somewhat modifying his attitude when it had become clear that he had successfully prevented a new and consolidated centralised Germany from arising.

When the struggle died down, as one may say, of exhaustion (it had been of a most abominable ferocity and had utterly ruined German wealth—the Germans did not recover for a century), the final settlement may properly be said to be Richelieu's work, though Richelieu himself had been dead for six years. Its date is 1648, and it was called the Peace of Westphalia. It left the Germans divided very much as they now are, into Catholic and Protestant; and, regarded as an attempt to restore religious unity among them, the Thirty Years' War was a failure. It was the last failure in the long list of the attempts to recover the unity of Christendom which had gone to pieces during the century before.

After the Peace of Westphalia the religious frontiers harden and become permanent, and the full disruption of Europe is achieved.

CHAPTER VIII

The Result

WE are now in a position to recapitulate the general movement of the Reformation, to tabulate the causes at work and the general dates of the process.

I postulated in my first chapter that these forces cannot be fully analysed. No one of the great movements of history can be so analysed, for each includes not only elements which are beyond any one man's degree of knowledge as an historian, but also elements which are beyond the experience or knowledge of all men: forces outside this world.

This is particularly true of the Reformation. You will not discover in mere terrestrial history anything sufficient to account for the catastrophe. All we can do is to capitulate the known factors at work, emphasising at the same time the seen forces not proceeding directly from human actions or will which presided over the whole.

Of the known factors, then, we have these:

1. There has been opposed to the Catholic Church from its foundation a spirit quite different from mere reaction against what is strong or organised. It is a special personal hatred of the Faith. This spirit in-

variably appears in every movement of schism or even of criticism. The moment (and wherever) the Church is fighting, that malign spirit appears. It had appeared on Calvary; it appears throughout the succeeding centuries; it appeared at once after the beginning of the Revolt in the early sixteenth century.

I say we must emphasise this first factor because the mass of our official historians ignore it.

2. The Revolt was originally and essentially a protest against two things: the spiritual power of the clergy; the financial power of the hierarchy and its chief, the Pope, and of the monastic orders. The two protests were inextricably mixed because the same man who was offended by exclusive spiritual power was also offended by large revenues drawn from his labour and enjoyed by an institution which in his eyes was no longer fulfilling its functions.

In other words, the Reformation was originally an anti-clerical movement much more than it was an anti-doctrinal movement, and so far from being a rationalist movement it led men away from rationalism into the opposite, dependence in a text and blind acceptance of merely affirmed, though various, unreasoned doctrines.

3. This movement was provoked by the very corrupt condition into which the official Church had fallen, notably the Papal court. The evil was neither universal nor of one quality; it fluctuated with time and place. There is no doubt, for instance, that St.

Albans (to quote an example of one monastery) was in a bad way years before the outbreak, while Glastonbury was sound. No one can deny the spiritual excellence of the first Borgia Pope, nor the gross immorality and scandal of the second. There were provinces of Christendom (and England was the most conspicuous) in which such evils as Pluralism and that fatal disease, the lay acquisition of endowments, were comparatively slight; there were others, like Scotland, immediately at hand, where they were enormous. But the contrast between what the official Church should have been—its holy functions—and what the official Church was, shocked men profoundly, and they were quite right to be shocked.

In general, the immediate spur which provoked the rebellion was the gross insufficiency of those responsible for the good name of the Church.

4. There was ready to hand for the support of any spiritual revolt a new doctrine of unquestioned right in Princes to absolute rule, coupled with a new doctrine, very shaky, but warmly supported, that General Councils were the supreme authority of the Church.

Helping all this was the practical weakening of the Papacy, through the Popes first leaving Rome and living almost as subjects of the French King up to 1377, and after that, for all the useful part of a lifetime, appearing as rivals, always two, sometimes three, one against the other. This was the Great Schism: a condition which led rival Popes to bid for support from the Princes, and made those Princes stronger than ever.

5. Meanwhile there governed the whole movement as a powerful and unceasing motive the chance presented to territorial lords, large and small, from kings down to squires, of looting Church property. This property was everywhere very large (too large for its function, especially since the Black Death) — in Scotland reputed to be half, in England from a third to a fifth, of the wealth of the governing classes, and elsewhere on the same scale. It was this opportunity for loot which worked the Reformation in England and Scotland, and prevented, in England at least, any permanent retracing of the steps taken. It was this same opportunity for loot which let loose the German nobles in a pack against religion, and which provoked in the main the French nobles to their prolonged rebellion.

Such are the main factors at work. The process may conveniently be divided into the successive divisions which these pages have followed.

(a) From 1517 to 1547-49 may be called the Period of Debate, which is also the period of flux, when the whole quarrel is boiling and nothing has yet crystallised. The English King breaks with the Pope, probably with no intention of making the breach permanent, and only over a personal point; but he dies in 1547 with the breach still unrepaired. What is much more important, he had looted the monastic lands, and yet was too weak to hold them. The loot was seized by the courtiers old and new and their hangers-on. In France, the Huguenot opposition has power, although no one has yet taken arms. In Germany, where the revolt began, there has been the most trouble, but it has only been made possible through the hampering of the Emperor (in his attempt to force order) by the Turkish peril at his gates.

This Period of Debate or chaotic discussion produced, rather more than half-way through its course (in 1536), a novel instrument, later to prove of the greatest power: the book of Jean Cauvin (whom we call John Calvin). This Frenchman produced a logical system of theology whereby men could get rid of the priest at the expense of free will, reintroduced the old terror of doom, and lent form to the fury which had arisen against the Catholic Church. All consistent Protestantism derives from him, and has for its essential conceptions: first, the isolation of the soul, with no intermediaries between itself and its Creator; secondly, the absence of any but one Will in the universe, and, therefore, a universal fate.

(b) The second period is much shorter; it is one, roughly, of a decade, 1549 to 1559-60. The men who were young at the beginning of the outbreak are growing old; the forces are lining up for Battle. The King of France, who had combated heresy, died and is succeeded by boys, vicious and weak, so that there is an opportunity for civil war. In England there is a period of further violent loot during the first half of the decade, and an attempted but not whole-hearted restoration of Catholicism during the second half. In Germany prolonged antagonisms have led to a sort of compromise, in which *for the first time since the threat of a break-up was made, those in revolt are recognised and allowed to separate themselves from the unity of Europe.*

(c) The third period in the process is yet another decade, or thereabouts, from 1559-60 to 1570-72. In England the power has been seized by the clique of New Millionaires who owe their position to the loot of the Church lands, and clerical wealth of all kinds. Cecil is their real head, and Elizabeth their figure-head—much against her will (save that she desires to remain on the throne). In France the gentry arm to obtain that loot which the Crown has hitherto forbidden them, but as the Crown is now only a succession of weak boys, they have their chance and raise civil war. In Scotland the English Government of Cecil has succeeded in its plans, the Lords, who in that country have ruined the Church to their own financial advantage, are completely in power; the Catholic queen is first a fugitive to, and then a close prisoner in, England. The period ends with a popular rising in Paris (the massacre of St. Bartholomew), which in effect renders impossible for the future the claim of the Protestant gentry to rule the country. It ends in England with a great Catholic rising in the north, which is suppressed with the utmost barbarity, and is followed by the excommunication of Elizabeth by the Pope. Meanwhile, in the Netherlands, the

great merchants and the principal territorial mag-
nates, backed by strong local feeling against Spain,
have begun an active rebellion and are approaching
success.

(d) The last phase in all countries begins in 1570-
1572 and lasts for anything between twenty-five and
thirty-five years. In the northern part of the Netherlands (which we now call Holland) the few nobles
and more powerful great merchants and money
dealers achieve their independence from Spain and
establish a rigid persecuting of Calvinism, though a
very large minority of their people are still Catholics.
The majority of the Provinces remain fully Catholic
and politically attached to Spain; to-day we call them
Belgium.

In England the rigid government of the wealthy
organised minority, led by William Cecil and his son
Robert after him, succeeds. Mary Queen of Scots,
the Catholic heiress to the throne, is put to death,
the rebels against Spain in the Netherlands are supported, a Spanish expedition to succour the Catholic
Church in England fails, and at the death of Queen
Elizabeth, in 1603, perhaps half the people are detached from Catholic tradition; two years after, the
Gunpowder Plot, nursed by the second Cecil, turns
the tide. After that date, 1605, the mass of England
becomes definitely anti-Catholic, and the essential
part of the struggle may be said to be over.

In France popular feeling makes the preponderance of the armed Protestant nobles incapable of gov-

erning the country. The legitimate heir to the throne, Henry of Bourbon, King of Navarre, though leader of the Protestant nobles and gentry, formally accepts Catholicism; but he establishes a compromise called the Edict of Nantes, whereby the very rich and powerful Protestant body is made a State within the State, given strongholds of its own, governed by its own nobles, and accorded legal and educational privileges of every kind.

By the end of the sixteenth and the beginning of the seventeenth century, therefore, the shipwreck of Western Christendom is complete; a permanent division is established in France, and in the Netherlands; England is separated from unity, and its Government permanently fixed as an anti-Catholic force, now followed by the mass of the people.

But there follows in Germany a very vigorous attempt to re-establish Catholic unity through the action of the Emperor. It is checked by the action of the French Minister, Richelieu, who helps the Protestants against the Emperor's efforts to make all Germany Catholic and united under his rule. The Peace of Westphalia in 1648 is the final settlement, after which the religious frontiers remain much what they are to this day. Such was the sequence of the mighty process which destroyed the common culture of Europe.

Its results were twofold: its effect upon character, and the consequent effect upon external life.

How the Reformation Happened

The effect of the Reformation on character was, where it succeeded, to isolate the soul. On this two important consequences follow.

The first was this: the corporate quality of society was shaken, where the Reformation succeeded. A process of disintegration took place, which might be compared to the breaking up of stiff soil by the plough and its falling into dust under the action of frost. The corporate sense which bound individuals together as in the old Guilds, in the old domestic social system, in the old forms of village life, was gradually, though only very gradually, dissolved. At the same time, and as consequence of this, individual energy was released. The principle of competition emerged more and more as time proceeded, and, with it, there arrived a force which is only to-day beginning to be analysed and its profound effects appreciated: Usury, that is, the taking of profit on an *unproductive* loan, a system which drains wealth from the many or the few and gives preponderant power to capital. Usury [1] was no new thing introduced by the Reformation, it is as old as the world and there was plenty of it in the Catholic culture of the Middle Ages. But the regarding of it as legitimate, normal and even beneficent was new and was the product of the breakdown in the old moral authority coupled with Calvin's doctrine of man's duty to grow rich. Before the Reformation the taking of interest on an

[1] It is important to remember that the amount of the interest has nothing to do with its being Usurious. One thousand per cent on a successful mining venture is not Usury. Three per cent on a War Loan is.

unproductive loan—the levying of a tax on industry for the benefit of capital whether used or no—was done, but was done by subterfuge as a thing known to be evil. After the Reformation it was the shirking of such interest which became wrong and dishonourable.

Under these twin forces of competition and usury the Protestant culture of Europe obtained an economic leadership. It was copied at a distance, imperfectly, later by the Catholic culture over which it had thus acquired a start it has not yet wholly lost. The Protestant States, notably England and Holland, begin a more active banking and trading, and a more intensive production, which later grows into what is called to-day Industrial Capitalism.

Here an important distinction must be made. The great advance in our physical powers over nature and in our knowledge of physical cause and effect is not a product of the Reformation at all: it is a product of the Renaissance. The Renaissance was not completed by, nor did it march side by side with, the Reformation; nor was the Reformation even a fruit of the Renaissance. The Reformation was essentially a diversion of the main stream of the Renaissance into narrower, incongruous channels, flowing in a different direction from that which the mighty stream of rediscovered culture would have followed, had it been left undisturbed.

We see this particularly in the strange delay imposed by the Reformation, *and* by the Catholic reaction against it, upon the progress of physical science. Tycho Brahe is turned out of a Protestant University for teaching the motion of the earth. Bacon ridicules such teaching. Even in the Catholic world Galileo is only allowed to teach it as an hypothesis and is condemned for teaching it as a truth, a fact which had been proved (in point of fact, it had not yet been proved). Such an attitude towards discovery would have been impossible to the old Humanist spirit of the pre-Reformation century.

This character of the Reformation as a diversion, not a product, of the Renaissance is still more noticeable in the field of art and particularly of Architecture. It is not till our own day, from three to four centuries later, that the uninterrupted use of the reason has been, by some, resumed. During most of the interval the mind of Europe has been halted by false authority, and even to-day it is astonishing to note how strong in the Protestant culture is the authority of mere print.

In a word, the modern material progress of Europe was not advanced by the Reformation. That progress sprang from the Renaissance. The degrading of the Renaissance into a religious quarrel deflected and warped the main development of our civilisation. But the Reformation did produce a special form in the general progress of instruments and physical science. This special form is, as I have said, Industrial Capitalism, with which all Europe to-day is actively at issue. It cannot be called a fortunate result.

The Result

The second important consequence of the isolation of the soul was subjectivism in philosophy. Subjectivism means (in this general popular sense of the word—I am not using it technically) referring to the individual for the test of truth. There is a sense, of course, in which we must all do that; for instance, a man accepting the authority of the reason, or of his senses, or of the Catholic Church, is necessarily exercising an individual judgment. But subjectivism rather signifies that the mind suffering from it (for it is a disease) questions what is corporate and general in authority, and prefers what is particular and isolated.

For instance, in the most important matter of all —Religion—he will take as the test of truth not the corporate authority of the Church, or even of natural religion as expressed by the tradition of mankind, but his own "Religious experience," as he calls it. This is so true that the man suffering from subjectivism becomes at last quite blind to the meaning of the word *Credo*—"I believe." He confuses Faith with a personal emotion, or visual concept. He cannot understand it as the acceptation on the word of an Authority, only accepted by the reason, of an objective truth which the individual may, or may not, have experienced as a personal emotion.

The result of this is that, as the few remaining Catholic dogmas accepted in the Protestant culture are abandoned one by one, society falls spiritually into the same sort of lust into which it fell socially through the same agency; and each man's standards differ potentially from his neighbour's. There supervenes a philosophic anarchy such as that into which we are now already plunged; with these results on morals, art, war, building and all social relations which we see around us.

But since man must worship something, the worship of humanity at large, and of the nation in particular—that is, the worship by the individual of himself in an extended form—takes the place of religion, and hence, politically, one of the supreme results of the Reformation has been the growth of Nationalism.

By this I do not mean that patriotism is a novelty, still less that it is other than a noble and exalted devotion. It is as old as civilised human society, and is, if not a virtue, the nearest thing to a virtue which we can find outside the field of pure Ethics. But I mean that making humanity the *end,* or even one's own nation the *end,* of action, is an error and a necessary seed of disaster. Indeed, to-day, from these two emotions of the worship of Humanity and the worship of the Nation, the very life of the world is imperilled.

It may be said that the Reformation, having these results, produced them only locally: that the Catholic culture was saved, and that it is still, in its general spirit, the test of civilisation. A European people or individual is, other things being equal, more civilised in proportion as it or he is more Catholic. That is true. But you cannot quite destroy the community of Christendom; and whatever powerfully affects one part of it must still, in different degrees, affect every part of it. Moreover, although the Catholic culture was saved, and although it still colours the mass of Christendom, yet it was itself wounded. I have shown how in France the anti-Catholic forces let loose in the sixteenth century have ever since been very powerful in that pivotal country, and have, over great spaces of time (the last forty or fifty years is an example), captured the Government, with all the enormous powers a modern Government has of imposing its doctrine upon its subjects by compulsory education and through the action of the Courts.

Similarly, among the German states and cities, the Catholic cause was wounded; it had failed to hold itself intact. The secessionists from Christendom succeeded in establishing themselves; the initiative lay with them for more than two hundred years. That is why you get the decline of Vienna and the rise of Berlin, and that is why, though numerically men of German speech are almost exactly half and half, Catholic and anti-Catholic, yet in the row of great modern German names in literature, science and philosophical speculation, by far the greater number and the most prominent are drawn from the culture opposed to Catholicism.

I conclude my brief Study of the Reformation by the remark that the Tide has turned in Europe. By which I do not mean to prophesy that the Catholic

Church will re-assume, even within so brief a space as two hundred years, that full empire over the minds of Western men which it held for so many centuries, and which caused us to become the head of the world. Indeed, I should think it more probable that the results of the Reformation would continue in a changed form and leave us still divided into a Catholic culture growing in strength and a strong, permanent, Pagan opposition thereto. But I mean when I say "the tide has turned" that the old process of perpetual retreat on the Catholic side, the old tiresome, defensive note in apologetics, the ambient idea that, somehow or other, the non-Catholic culture was always more prosperous materially and more successful in arms—all this is being reversed. In England and Scotland, and in the New World of English speech (save where it is spoken by men of Irish, Italian, Polish or South German stock), this truth will be appreciated more slowly than elsewhere. But on the Continent of Europe and in the world at large, it is already manifest.

It is apparent in the things of the mind, where the Catholic position has taken on a note of superiority, and where it is the anti-Catholic who is thrown upon the defensive. It is apparent politically in the powerful resurrection of Catholic societies, such as Poland and Ireland, and the strengthening of older ones, such as Italy. It is apparent in that subtle thing, intellectual fashion. Not that I quote it for praise, but only as a symptom. The young man in Paris to-day who wants to be thought advanced claims some reading of St. Thomas. It would have been an attitude so eccentric as to seem mad a lifetime ago.

What the end will be we cannot tell. Probably conflict. But there is no doubt at all of the change. It was high time!

Index

Index

Index

Index

Index

Index

Index

Index

Index

Index

Index

Index

Index

Index

Index